# LETTING FRENCH PROPERTY SUCCESSFULLY

**Stephen Smith and Charles Parkinson**

LETTING FRENCH PROPERTY SUCCESSFULLY

# Letting French Property Successfully

## © *Stephen Smith and Charles Parkinson*

*ISBN 0-9511991-4-5*

*Published by:*
PKF (Guernsey) Limited
PO Box 296, St Peter Port, Guernsey GY1 4NA
Telephone: 01481 727927. Facsimile: 01481 710511

Typeset and design by PKF (Guernsey) Ltd
and Avonset, Bath
Printed in Great Britain by Cromwell Press Ltd, Trowbridge, Wiltshire
Third Edition

**Disclaimer**

The information contained in this book is offered as a basis for further consideration only and is not to be acted upon without independent advice from suitably qualified professionals based on the actual circumstances of the taxpayer.

Neither the publisher nor the author can accept any responsibility for any loss occasioned to any person no matter howsoever caused or arising as a result of or in consequence of action taken or refrained from in reliance on the contents of this book.

# WHERE TO GO FOR FURTHER ADVICE AND INFORMATION

Although all the main issues are considered in this book, it is impossible to discuss every subject in detail within this format and this book should not therefore be considered as exhaustive and sufficient in itself to make investment decisions. Professional advice should be sought in connection with specific cases and the issues arising from them. Neither the publisher nor the authors can accept any responsibility for any loss occasioned to any person no matter howsoever caused or arising as a result of or in consequence of action taken or refrained from in reliance on the contents of this book.

If you would like more advice or information on French property and related matters, please contact **Stephen Smith** or **Keith Croft** at:

> **Riddell Croft & Co**
> 27 St Helen's Street,
> Ipswich IP4 4HH
> Tel: (01473) 384870
> Fax: (01473) 384878
> (International dialling code: 44 1473)

For further information on French tax and related matters, please contact **Charles Parkinson** or **Virginie Deflassieux** at:

> **PKF (Guernsey) Ltd**
> P O Box 296
> St Peter Port
> Guernsey GY1 4NA
> Tel: (01481) 727927
> Fax: (01481) 710511
> (International dialling code: 44 1481)

# CONTENTS

# INTRODUCTION

In recent years, thousands of UK families or groups of friends have bought a property in France to escape from cold winters and wet summers. For many, their personal use of the property is a source of considerable pleasure. Although by British standards property prices in France are still generally low, and purchase loans are readily available, many potential buyers are discouraged from purchasing French property for two main reasons. Firstly, they do not want to feel tied down to the same property each year when there are other countries or parts of France to explore. Secondly, their available holiday time is often limited to two or three weeks in the summer and, although friends and relatives may occasionally visit the property, it will otherwise remain unoccupied for the rest of the year.

On the other hand, more than 25 million tourists visit France each year. This is not a passing phenomenon and with new, improved and cheaper transport links, the demand for self-catering accommodation in France continues to grow from foreign holidaymakers, especially in Britain and northern Europe.

The purpose of this book is to provide a guide to the main practical, legal and tax processes necessary to let your property successfully in France. It reflects the current laws as at 31 October 2000 and explains how, in the short term, the rent you charge might not only cover annual maintenance and other expenses, but also leave you with surplus income to pay for your own holiday. With careful planning, more systematic lettings could also earn you enough income to recover your initial capital outlay and borrowings. You may even decide to buy more property to let as a business!

# 1.   PRACTICAL CONSIDERATIONS

## 1.1   CHOOSING THE LOCATION

Although landlords ('you') and your tenants will be welcome in most *communes*, many properties in France have no letting potential. As a landlord, your choice of property should be dictated by what your tenants are likely to want. For example, a converted barn in a beautiful, peaceful but remote part of France is less likely to attract regular tenants than a well-furnished property which is within fairly easy reach of shops, restaurants and other tourist attractions.

Under the French Planning Code, properties located in Paris, within 50 kilometres of 'ancient Parisian fortifications' and in *communes* with a population of at least 10,000 inhabitants cannot be converted into furnished lettings if the landlord is classed as a 'professional' (see 7.2.5). Some other *communes* in France have voluntarily adopted the same restriction and the position should always therefore be carefully checked if you are intending to let furnished property in France as a 'professional'. However, the French Planning Code states that this restriction will not apply to properties in areas of France which are 'habitually let out in the holiday season' (eg seaside, ski or spa resorts).

The tourist industry in some parts of France is estimated to have dropped by up to 30% in recent years. Most *départements* have a tourist office whose English-speaking staff can supply information free of charge on all aspects of tourism within their region. The French Government Tourist Board in London (Tel: 0891 244123) may also be able to help.

Demand for properties starts earliest in coastal parts of France, especially the Vendée and Charente Maritime; followed by Normandy and Brittany, Provence and Languedoc-Roussillon. The season for inland regions start a little later.

Inland regions tend to experience extremes of temperature with hot summers and freezing winters, whereas north of the Loire valley and along the Atlantic coast, the climate is similar to Britain. Many tourists are drawn to the south and (cheaper) south-west regions of France which usually enjoy hot dry periods lasting unbroken from early spring till late autumn, and cool dry winters. First choice is usually for properties with private swimming pools. The investment return in a swimming pool can be recovered in a very short time.

Apart from climatic factors, distance and ease of travel are important considerations. Properties in Brittany and Normandy are often in demand because tenants (especially those with young families) can reach them without travelling long distances. There is no doubt that the Channel Tunnel has made access to North-Eastern France and the main *autoroutes* to the South much easier. Many properties are also within easy reach of a daily air, rail or motorail connection, although some services do not operate at weekends, or only operate in the summer. Whatever the weather, many properties located in the mountains or close to ski resorts have an all year-round letting potential.

## 1.2    CHOOSING THE PROPERTY

Although a newly-built property is generally easier and cheaper to maintain, an older property which has been well modernised and equipped is more likely to appeal to tenants.

A local French estate agent (*agent immobilier*) or letting agent (*agent de location*) may, without charge or obligation, help you find a property with letting potential and advise on the likely rent that may be achieved. French estate agents will not usually supply a list of properties for sale and their particulars tend to be brief and handwritten without a colour photograph or room dimensions. Money can be saved and fruitless visits avoided by instructing a recommended British agent specialising in French property to help you find a suitable property in your chosen region of France.

If you own a flat, villa or other property forming part of a larger development, the *règlement de copropriété* or internal regulations should be checked to ensure that there are no restrictions on your ability to let the property. In some cases, you must obtain written consent to let the property from the *syndic* or managing agent of the development. Even if there are no restrictions on letting, it is always prudent for insurance reasons to supply the *syndic* with written details of the periods when the property will be occupied and by whom.

The letting agreement should oblige the tenant to observe all the internal regulations and he should therefore be supplied with a copy of the relevant parts of the *règlement de copropriété* (with an English-language translation if necessary) before he takes occupation.

## 1.3    BUDGETING

You should budget for legal and survey fees; annual taxes and outgoings; transport costs to and from the property, furniture, maintenance and renovation expenses.

### 1.3.1    *Purchase and ownership costs*

Your vendor will normally pay the estate agent's commission, but it is customary for the buyer to pay the legal fees and duties relating to the purchase. The legal fees charged by a *Notaire* or French property lawyer are currently calculated as follows:

| Bands | % |
|---|---|
| 0 to 20,000 | 5 |
| 20,000 to 40,000 | 3.3 |
| 40,000 to 110,000 | 1.65 |
| 110,000 upwards | 0.825 |

French VAT ('TVA') at 19.6% is paid on the purchase of a new property. A sale of a building will be subject to TVA either if the property is sold before it is completed; or if it is sold within 5 years of its completion, not having previously been sold by a non-trader. When the property acquired is less than 5 years old, TVA is paid by the vendor, but in practice this means that it is added to the sale price.

If the property is more than 5 years old, no TVA is payable, but the transaction is subject to stamp duties (*droits d'enregistrement*). The element of this tax paid to the *département* was around 5% but has been reduced to 3.6% as from 15 September 1999. In addition, an element of 1.2% is paid to the local *commune*. In all, stamp duties total 4.8% and are payable by the purchaser unless the parties agree otherwise.

When a building plot is acquired (or the property consists of buildings to be demolished to make way for new construction) the purchase is subject to TVA at the normal rate – which is usually borne by the purchaser. The transfer is also subject to a 'publicity tax' of 0.6% based on the net of TVA value. Work performed by building contractors is normally subject to TVA at 19.6%. In larger communities there may be an additional building tax of between 1 and 5%.

Certain improvement, transformation, or maintenance works carried out on residential property over two years old may be subject to a reduced TVA rate of 5.5%. This TVA reduction applies until 31 December 2002.

### 1.3.2    Local taxes

The *taxes foncières* or local land and property taxes are levied on the owner of French property each year, calculated by reference to its theoretical rental value set by the local *cadastre* or land registry. New or renovated properties are generally exempt from these taxes for 2 years commencing on 1 January following the date of their structural completion, provided the work undertaken has been declared within 90 days of its completion. A *taxe d'habitation* charge is also payable each year by the occupier (owner or tenant) of any property suitable for residential occupation. If the letting is seasonal, the owner is more likely to pay the *taxe d'habitation*. In some parts of France, sundry taxes or *taxes assimilées* will also be charged by the local authority for the supply of snow sweeping or other amenities. These taxes are usually lower than similar charges in the UK.

### 1.3.3    Other outgoings

You will be responsible for the cost of electricity, gas, water, telephone and other supplies from the date of completion of your purchase. If you own a flat, you will also be liable for the cost of annual maintenance and service charges. You should also budget for compulsory buildings and contents insurance premiums (see 3.7).

## 1.4    RAISING FINANCE

There are two ways in which you can raise finance to purchase residential property in France. The most popular way is to borrow in French Francs from a French bank or other lender. As a general rule, French lenders will allow you to borrow up to 80% of the purchase price and improvement costs over a term of between 5 and 15 years. The loan will not usually include mortgage arrangement fees, legal fees and attendant purchase expenses. Monthly repayments are usually made by direct debit from a French bank account which you will be asked to open prior to completing the loan. Life assurance cover is usually also required. If you need to borrow money to improve or renovate the property, it is advisable to apply for a mortgage before you buy the property as French banks will not always lend you the necessary funds once you own the property.

If you take out a loan on the security of a French property, a further registration fee of between 1% and 2% of the monies borrowed will be charged and it may therefore be more cost effective to borrow from a financial institution in your own country by creating a charge over or remortgaging your main residence, or offering other assets as security for the loan.

When applying for a loan, some banks will ask you for a cash flow forecast detailing anticipated capital and income expenses and the rental income you expect to earn.

If the property is mortgaged, it is essential that written permission for the letting is obtained from the building society or bank which granted the mortgage. They may have a standard form of notice which will have to be signed by both the landlord and the prospective tenant. The building society or bank may also charge a higher rate of interest as the letting may be regarded as a commercial arrangement.

# 2. THE PURCHASE PROCESS AND OWNERSHIP STRUCTURING

## 2.1 THE IMPORTANCE OF TAKING EARLY INDEPENDENT PROFESSIONAL ADVICE

French estate agents often invite you to sign their own pre-printed contract. It is very important not to sign anything without legal advice. Some contracts bear English translations, but many are misleading or unintelligible. Having French documents translated into English is not enough. The contract should also be checked to establish whether, in addition to the purchase price, you will also be liable to pay the estate agent's commission. What has been left out of a French document can be just as important as its contents. Once you have signed a contract, you are almost always bound to complete the purchase. Before signing a contract, you should therefore ensure that it truly records what you have agreed and contains all the appropriate clauses for your protection. If not, you lose the opportunity to insert your own tailor-made requirements. If a dispute arises, you must instruct an *avocat* or barrister specialising in contentious work. Many foreign purchasers have found themselves involved in expensive legal proceedings in France because they were unable or unwilling to complete a transaction and were not fully aware of the terms of their contract.

Transfers of real property (land and buildings) in France have to be witnessed by a public official called a *Notaire*. In some cases, the *Notaire* also acts as an estate agent, and may have drawn up the contract, but it is not usual for him to be involved until after you have signed the contract and become legally bound to buy a property. The *Notaire* is often instructed to act for both the vendor and the purchaser. A purchaser has the right to choose his own separate *Notaire* and should not usually instruct the *Notaire* acting for the seller. Unlike a Solicitor, the *Notaire* is not appointed to represent your interests but acts as an intermediary for both parties to a French property transaction. As an independent official, his main duty of care is to ensure that the documents which legally transfer ownership of the property are in order. *Notaires* do not usually regard it as necessary to keep you informed about your purchase or mortgage application. They will not perform the role or give you the same security and protection as you would expect from an English Solicitor. Questions on many aspects of your transaction cannot be answered by lawyers and other professionals in France since they involve considerations of foreign law. For example, what happens to your English property if you die in France? Who pays what taxes, and to which country?

You should therefore approach every aspect of your French purchase with caution and seek proper advice at the earliest stages from bilingual lawyers in your home country who have the knowledge and experience to liaise with the *Notaire* by telephone or fax when the need arises and to advise on both French law and the interplay of French and English (or other foreign) law.

## 2.2 CONVEYANCING

French law does not recognise the concept of 'subject to contract' and, once you have chosen a property and agreed a purchase price, according to Article 1583 of the French Civil Code you have entered into a binding contract. In practice, you will be asked to sign a preliminary contract at this early stage. Before you make any legal commitment, you should consider obtaining a structural survey report and valuation. Your vendor does not usually have to disclose any structural defects affecting the property. This means that if, after signing a contract, you discover structural or other defects to the property and its equipment/services, you are still obliged to complete the purchase at the agreed price and cannot obtain compensation from your vendor.

You should also obtain an up-to-date registered plan or *plan cadastral* of the property which shows the extent and boundaries of the property. Legal advice should be taken if this is not clear. It is prudent to check the legal title and other documents for rights of way and other easements which might adversely affect your enjoyment of the property, and whether planning permission or some other consent was/will be required for any construction or change to the external aspect or permitted user of the property. Planning permission (see 3.1) is sometimes required if you want to install a swimming pool, septic tank, or improvement works to the interior of the property. The property or the area in which it is situated may be protected in some way, in which case it is an offence to make any alterations or improvements without first obtaining a special type of planning permission. There may be other matters which, although not visible, could adversely affect your use and enjoyment of the property. In every case, proper enquiries and searches should be made.

There are two main forms of contract. The more common type is a *compromis de vente* which is an agreement signed by both parties and subsequently reiterated before the *Notaire* by a deed of sale called an *acte de vente*. In some parts of France, the transaction is recorded in a one-sided document called a *promesse de vente*. Whatever the type of contract used, it should not be signed before you have had it thoroughly checked and approved.

When the contract has been signed by the buyer a deposit of 10% of the purchase price is payable. If the property is less than 5 years old the deposit will be 5%. This is deposited with the *Notaire* witnessing the conveyance, or the estate agent if he is authorised to accept deposits. The deposit is a part payment of the purchase price if the contract is completed, but it is forefeited if the buyer withdraws from the contract, and the seller must usually pay the buyer the same amount in damages (as well as refunding the deposit) if he withdraws from the contract. The contract will usually contain conditions, such as that it is subject to the buyer obtaining finance; if these conditions are not fulfilled the deposit is refundable. Because of the penalty of the amount of the deposit, it is rare to see sellers breaking a sale agreement to accept a higher offer.

Once the conveyancing documents have been completed by the *Notaire*, normally after 4-8 weeks, the buyer is asked to pay to the *Notaire* the balance of the purchase price. The *Notaire* is personally liable for the registration taxes on the sale and will also insist on having these and his costs before proceeding. The buyer and seller have to be present before the *Notaire*, in person or by giving a Power of Attorney, for the signature of the *acte de vente*.

If the property to be acquired is unfinished, the parties will sign a reservation contract and the purchaser will pay a deposit of 5% if the property is to be completed within a year, 2% if the property is to be completed within 1-2 years and no deposit if the property will be completed after more than 2 years.

## 2.3    BUYING A NEW PROPERTY IN FRANCE

If you buy a new flat, villa or other property (under construction or less than 5 years old) forming part of a larger development in France, the *Code de la Construction et de l'Habitation* should protect you if the developer goes bankrupt, or from other possible pitfalls.

### 2.3.1    *The Contract*

When you have decided on a property and agreed a price, the developer will – at an early stage – ask you to sign a *contrat de réservation* or *contrat préliminaire* (all other types of contract are void) and to pay a *réservation* (non-interest bearing deposit). If the building works are to be completed within one year of signing the contract, the deposit cannot exceed 5% (2% if within two years; no deposit if longer). The contract should – but often does not – provide:

a)  A full description and the approximate *surface habitable* of the *partie privative* (see last month's article);

b)  A layout plan (*plan de masse*) and a floor plan (*plan des locaux*) of the *partie privative*;

c)  A specification note (*notice technique sommaire*) giving details of the building materials and domestic services and fittings to be provided. It is important that you fully understand this technical document to avoid any disappointment at a later stage when it would be difficult to change the specifications;

d)  If the purchase price is firm and final (in some cases the developer can increase it);

e)  The date by which the building works will have to be completed. A financial guarantee must be provided, either by the developer (*garantie intrensèque*) or by a third party (*garantie extrinsèque*). A prudent buyer will ensure that the latter is obtained. The third party guarantor must be an accredited financial institution that will arrange for the completion of building works or the refund of the purchase price in the event of the developer's failure to complete;

f) Any *conditions suspensives* (special conditions) you wish to add to the contract.

As explained in section 2.4 below, you should not sign the contract without having seen and studied the *réglement de copropriété* and the *état descriptif de division* (both technical documents) and have a good idea of the amount of annual maintenance and service charges you will have to pay.

A copy of the signed contract must be given to you before you make any payments. If you do not sign the contract in from of a *notaire,* it will only become legally binding seven days after you have received a copy of the contract by registered letter which can be proved by acknowledgement of receipt ('LRAR'). In this time, you may usually withdraw from the contract if you serve written notice on the developer by LRAR. Any complaints you may have throughout the building programme should also be sent to the developer by fax and/or LRAR.

### 2.3.2 Completion

You will eventually receive a statutory notice asking you to complete the purchase, together with a draft (*project*) of the *acte de vente* (transfer deed).

You complete your purchase by signing the transfer deed which conveys ownership to you of the – usually incompleted – *partie privative* and *parties communes*. You automatically acquire ownership of the rest of your property – for which you pay installments of the purchase price – as the building works progress. Stage payments are usually made as follows:

- 35% on completion of the foundations;

- 35% on the building being made watertight;

- 25% on completion of the building.

When the property is fit for occupation, you will be asked for the last stage payment. Provided the building work is generally completed as specified in the contract, then you must accept it. Only a substantial defect would entitle you to withhold the last payment. French law allows a reasonable delay for completion of landscaping and other ancillary works.

From the day the keys are handed over, there is a one-month guarantee period against visible structural defects. French law also provides you with a 10-year warranty against latent defects which affect the structure of the building including those resulting from subsoil conditions. All those involved in the building programme may be liable unless it can be proved that the damage was caused by something outside their control. There is also a 2-year warranty against defects in equipment (e.g. central heating) in the building.

Whilst France sets a high standard for the protection of purchasers of new property, there are still many pitfalls. To avoid these, it is essential to take proper advice at an early stage of your purchase from someone will versed in the legal technicalities involved.

## 2.4 BUYING A FLAT

There are many advantages (and rental income opportunities) to owning a French flat which, in holiday resorts or cities, is often the most affordable option.

As a *copropriétaire*, you do not buy a lease in a development but own the freehold to (a) the *partie* privative – flat, storage room, garage etc., designated for you exclusive use – and; (b) a share of the *parties communes* – staircases, lifts, gardens, swimming pool etc., - for which all *copropriétaires* (who are jointly responsible for their maintenance and upkeep) must pay service charges.

By signing the French purchase contract, you are legally bound by the *règlement de copropriété* ('RDC') which contains all the rules and your liabilities relating to the management, upkeep and appearance of the development. You should therefore insist on having sight of a full registered copy of this important document before you commit yourself to a purchase. Even if you speak fluent French, you are unlikely to understand this technical document without bilingual legal assistance.

The RDC contains a detailed description of your property, stipulating which parts are private and which are common (balconies and other parts of a development can be either). Generally, *copropriétaires* can only use their *partie privative* for private residential – i.e. non-commercial – purposes. The position should however always be checked. There are cases of buyers taking flats near property which, although originally residential in user, became fishmongers, nightclubs or other similar nuisances.

The RDC also provides 'house rules' and regulates the permitted external appearance of your property (e.g. blinds, exterior paintwork and drying clothes on balconies). There will be restrictions on where you or your guests can park cars. The French courts may modify the provisions of an RDC which are unreasonably restrictive or unfair.

All *copropriétaires* automatically and compulsorily become members of a *syndicat* which is responsible for the development. Usually, a *syndic* (professional manager) is appointed to be responsible for the day-to-day running of the development. He is often assisted in a consultative capacity by a management committee (*conseil syndical*) comprised of *copropriétaires*.

An annual general meeting must be held to approve the accounts for the previous year and to prepare a budget for the next year (if an important matter arises, an extraordinary general meeting can be convened). In both cases, 15 days' notice must be given together with the agenda. All *copropriétaires* can attend meetings which are held in French, and difficult to understand.

If voting rules have been properly followed, adopted resolutions are binding on all *copropriétaires.* The law specifies which type of voting must be used for different matters, e.g:

– simple majority for approval of annual accounts and budgets;

– absolute majority for appointment and dismissal of the *syndic*;

– unanimity for change of user and modification of allocation of service charges.

The insurance of the common parts of the development is the responsibility of the *copropriété* as a whole and is usually delegated to the *syndic*. The premiums will form part of the annual service charge made for the maintenance of the building. The insurance of the *partie privative* is the responsibility of each *copropriétaire.* It is an offence not to have minimum third party civil liability insurance by the date of completion. However, it is essential to consult the *syndic* before taking out insurance as it is becoming more and more common for *copropriétés* to effect insurance in respect of both the common and private parts of the development.

If you are thinking of letting your property, the RDC should be checked to ensure that there are no restrictions. In some cases, you must obtain written consent from the *syndic* to let your property. Even if there are no restrictions on letting, it is always prudent for insurance reasons to supply the *syndic* with written details of the periods when the property will be occupied and by whom.

Your (written) letting agreement should oblige the tenant to observe all the regulations and he should therefore be supplied with a copy of the relevant parts of the RDC (with an English language translation if necessary) before he takes occupation.

## 2.5   'LEASEBACK' PURCHASES

In some new French property developments, the developer offers a reduction in the purchase price of up to 40% in exchange for the purchaser leasing the property back to the developer for most of the year. The VAT on the purchase price may also be refunded to the investor in such cases, resulting in a considerable saving on the total price. A further benefit of a purchase structured in this way is that the purchaser is deemed to have paid the full price (net of VAT if this has been refunded), and his future capital gain therefore does not include the discount given to him by the developer.

The developer will let the property to tourists for the majority of the year, and the buyer retains the right to occupy the property rent-free for (usually) up to 6 weeks a year. The buyer may receive part of the rental income, depending on the terms of the agreement (and in particular on the level of discount the developer has given in the purchase price).

The conditions that must be fulfilled so that this apparently attractive arrangement achieves the desired fiscal and practical results are listed below, it being assumed, as will nearly always be the case, that the buyer has purchased a flat:

a)  The flat must be in a building which is *'classé'*. This means that it has to the satisfaction of the *Préfet* of the *département* in which it is situated complied with the regulations relating to properties let to tourists *('résidences de tourisme')*.

b)  The lease must be for at least 9 years. In addition at least 70% of the flats in the same building must be similarly let.

c)  The letting must be for the purposes of 'exploitation para-hôtelière' (the provision of hotel-like services) since lettings of property with no provision of food are exempt from VAT, and the buyer would not then get his VAT refund.

d)  The management company must undertake to promote French tourism abroad. In addition, during the first 2 years it must undertake to spend at least 1.5% of the income from the sub-lettings on seeking foreign tourists, or it must enter into contracts with tourist agencies to put at their disposal at least 20% of the available letting space.

e)  The management company will be required to keep the premises and its contents in a good state of repair and fully insured and to pay all taxes which would normally fall on a tenant. The buyer/landlord covenants to pay the service charges and taxes normally paid by an owner (including the *taxes foncières* and the *taxe d'habitation*) and to pay the management company a sum for its services.

f)   The management company pays rent at two rates, depending on whether the buyer is in occupation or not. The rent is linked to what the management company receives from its sub-lettings, and is usually paid annually in arrears.

At the end of the contract, the buyer is supposed to obtain vacant possession, however under French law the management company, as the lessee, has the right to the renewal of the lease. If the renewal is not granted, the tenant has a right to compensation. Since this does not form any part of the intentions of the parties at the outset, some management companies offer to indemnify the owner or to procure the indemnity of another company in their group in an amount equal to the amount to which the management company would be entitled on a refusal of a renewal. The difficulty is of course that the company providing the indemnity may have gone out of business in 9 year's time. The solution is to get the management company to execute a waiver of its rights (which cannot be done in the lease itself or at the same time as the lease is executed, so the buyer will be at risk for a short period). The buyer/landlord must also insist on the introduction of a clause into the lease prohibiting assignments of the lease without the consent of the landlord and requiring that the landlord is a party to any assignment so that he can impose the effect of the waiver on the assignee.

## 2.6 STRUCTURING YOUR OWNERSHIP

In many cases a non-resident buying property in France will be buying it jointly with his or her spouse, or in partnership with other non-residents. The purchasers will therefore be keen to arrange their ownership so that they each have appropriate rights to the property, particularly in the event of one of the co-owners dying. In the French tax system, individuals owning French property who are 'domiciled' (i.e. habitually resident) abroad are generally treated more favourably than companies which own property in France. However, as explained below, it may not be appropriate for you to own French property as individuals.

### 2.6.1 Ownership as individuals

The main forms of joint ownership are *indivision* and *tontine*. In practical terms, the difference is that when property is owned by two or more individuals *en indivision*, and one of them dies, his or her share devolves to his or her heirs under the rules of French succession law (see below). When property is owned *en tontine*, the survivor of the owners is deemed to have owned the whole property from the beginning.

An *indivision* can simply result from a succession.

In France, a deceased's assets do not pass to Executors (who distribute them in accordance with his Will), but immediately vest in his *réserve* and other beneficiaries *en indivision*; and the administration of the estate is in their hands. This can lead to serious family squabbles.

For example, if an *indivisaire* (co-owner *en indivision*) wants to sell his share of a French house to an outsider, he must give written notice to the other *indivisaire* (s) who can themselves purchase that share in place of the outsider. If an *indivisaire* cannot sell his share (at the price he wants) to the other *indivisaires* or to an outsider, the French courts can order that the whole of the property be sold without the consent of the other *indivisaires.* To avoid the above and other possible problems, *indivisaires* can enter into a binding *convention d'indivision* which regulates the use, management and devolution of the property.

However, a *convention* cannot avoid the following possible problem. If on an *indivisaire's* death one or more of his children is under 18 years of age (or any of his children have predeceased him leaving minor issue), the deceased's surviving spouse or other *indivisaire (s)* may not be able to sell or otherwise dispose of the property until the youngest of any minors reaches the age of majority. This is because minors cannot themselves sell French *immeubles*. If the minors are French domiciled, the French courts can in some cases authorise a surviving parent or other person to dispose of the minors' property in France. If the minors are domiciled in England, the French courts have no jurisdiction, and under English law the English courts cannot authorise a surviving parent, trustee or guardian to dispose of the minor's French property.

Most *notaires* issue no warning to English buyers about the problems of owning French property *en indivision*, which can usually be avoided or mitigated in a number of ways by taking advice from lawyers well versed in the laws of both countries, preferably before you acquire French property.

For example, it costs nothing to insert a *tontine* clause in the French conveyance when you acquire French *immeubles* (afterwards it is too late). This ensures that the property passes automatically to the surviving spouse, who is free to dispose of it as he or she wishes. Unfortunately, the *tontine* does not remove the exposure to French inheritance tax and when one of the co-owner dies, the tax is charged as if a half share of the property passes to the survivor. There is only one transferee, and therefore only one exemption to set against the value of the estate.

Another point to bear in mind is that if the parties of an *acquisition en tontine* subsequently fall out, the position can be extremely messy, and it may not be easy for one of the parties to extricate himself or herself from the investment.

Couples marrying in France enter into a contract regulating their property rights. 90% of them enter into a 'community property' marriage contract, under which part or all of their property is considered to be property of the marriage (whoever may be the registered owner). The French consider that a normal British marriage gives rise to a 'separate estates' marital regime, so that property registered in the name of one spouse belongs to that spouse. It is entirely possible, however, for a couple who have been married under foreign law for many years to form a French marriage contract in relation to their French property. This device can protect the surviving spouse, and saves French inheritance tax (see below 2.6.2).

### 2.6.2 French succession law and inheritance tax

French succession law prevents individuals from disposing of their French property exactly as they would wish. When you die, certain close relatives known as *héritiers réservataires* or entrenched heirs become entitled to a *réserve légale* or reserved share in the title to your French property as of right from the moment of your death. It is important to note that French property belonging to a deceased individual will **not** pass to his surviving spouse or partner under the entrenched heirship rules. This is partly explained by the fact that, normally, much of the property belonging to the spouses is 'community property' which may pass to the surviving spouse in any event (see 2.6.1 above).

In respect of the property which belonged to the deceased, if the deceased leaves one living child (or a deceased child with living issue), that child (or the grandchildren) is entitled to a share in one-half of the French property (as a minimum). If the deceased leaves two children or their issue, their reserved share is two-thirds. If there are three or more children or their issue, they share at least three-quarters. If the deceased leaves no children or other descendants but leaves surviving ascendants in both maternal and paternal lines, their reserved share is one-half of the French property. If the deceased leaves ascendants in one line only, they share in at least one-quarter of the property.

Provided that you make a valid Will, the *quotité disponible* or remainder of your French property can pass to your surviving spouse or any other beneficiary of your choosing. If you do not make a Will, the remainder of your French property may pass under French intestacy rules to more distant family relatives (e.g. brothers and sisters) and your surviving spouse will usually only have limited rights of ownership in your share of the property.

If you have already made a Will (English or French), it will be invalid to the extent that it gives to anyone else part of your estate which, under the rules of French succession law, must go to your *réservataires*. Although a French Will is not strictly necessary if your English Will complies with these rules, the administration of your French estate under an English Will can give rise to complex and costly formalities. For example, the Will must be translated into French and certified by a French court official, notarised, and its authority proven by lengthy French language affidavits of law.

To simplify the process, and reduce the cost of winding up your estate in France, it is usually preferable to execute an English Will which excludes all reference to your French property; and a French Will limited to your French property. If you decide not to make a French Will, the solicitor chosen to draw up your English Will should be aware of the French succession law and international taxation issues which will arise when you die.

A French Will can either be *authentique, olographe* or *secret* (this last form is rarely used). The main advantage of an *authentique* Will, which must be prepared by, executed and witnessed before one or two French *notaires,* is that the date on which it was made and the capacity of the person making it cannot be questioned. It can validly be made by a testator who cannot write because he is, for example, blind or infirm. By contrast, an *olographe* Will (which must be entirely in the handwriting of and signed and dated by the testator, and does not need to be witnessed) is much simpler and cheaper to prepare. It can be executed in England and no-one needs to know of its contents. Its main disadvantages are that the testator may not know how exactly to explain his wishes (so that it is open to various interpretations); and that it can easily be destroyed if left at home. These problems can be avoided by having its contents prepared in unambiguous terms by a lawyer, and depositing the executed original with a *notaire* who will register it at the Central Wills Registry in France.

Many *notaires* advise their English clients to execute a *donation entre époux* as a method of side-stepping and solving all the succession problems which French law can impose on them. However, it does not, and the formal documentation and expenses involved achieves nothing which is not achieved by making a French Will.

Most English and French Wills contain the clause "I revoke all former Wills". A recent case saw a lady lose the French property she would otherwise have inherited under her late husband's French Will because his English solicitor had drawn up a more recent English Will, unwittingly cancelling the original French Will. To avoid these and other possible problems which can lead to costly disputes, it is important that your two Wills are drafted in such a way that one does not revoke the other.

The French tax rules encourage people to leave French property to children, parents or spouses by allowing generous nil rate bands and lower rates of gift tax.

Couples married under a community property marriage regime will benefit from a 1% registration duty in lieu of normal inheritance tax rates if the community property passes to the surviving spouse.

Transfers of assets which are not part of a marriage community property, and between husband and wife are taxable in France, after a tax-free allowance of FrF 500,000. The rates applicable to the remainder are as follows:

| *Band of Value* | *Rate of Tax*<br>*%* |
| --- | :---: |
| Less than FrF 50,000 | 5 |
| FrF     50,000  to FrF     100,000 | 10 |
| FrF    100,000  to FrF     200,000 | 15 |
| FrF    200,000  to FrF  3,400,000 | 20 |
| FrF  3,400,000  to FrF  5,600,000 | 30 |
| FrF  5,600,000  to FrF 11,200,000 | 35 |
| FrF 11,200,000  upwards | 40 |

Transfers between ascendants and descendants or vice versa are taxed at the rates below after an abatement of FrF 300,000 per beneficiary:

| Band of Value | Rate of Tax % |
|---|---|
| Less than FrF 50,000 | 5 |
| FrF      50,000  to  FrF      75,000 | 10 |
| FrF      75,000  to  FrF     100,000 | 15 |
| FrF     100,000  to  FrF   3,400,000 | 20 |
| FrF   3,400,000  to  FrF   5,600,000 | 30 |
| FrF   5,600,000  to  FrF  11,200,000 | 35 |
| FrF  11,200,000  upwards | 40 |

Transfers between siblings are taxed as follows after an abatement of FrF 100,000 per beneficiary.

| Band of Value | Rate of Tax % |
|---|---|
| Less than FrF 150,000 | 35 |
| FrF 150,000 upwards | 40 |

Transfers to cousins and second cousins are taxed at 55% after an abatement of FrF 10,000.

Transfers to individuals not related by blood or marriage are taxed at 60%. The same rate applies to gifts to foreign charities, even though such gifts might have been exempt from tax in the country where the charity is based.

From 16 November 1999, unmarried couples may benefit from lower rates under the PACS or *Pacte Civil de Solidarité* arrangement. This is a contract concluded by two adults living together as a couple. The PACS is opened to both hetero-sexual and homosexual couples. The partners must not be closely related to each other, and neither of them may be already married or a partner in another PACS. If either partner becomes married to someone else, the PACS is dissolved. In terms of inheritance tax the partners in a PACS are entitled to an abatement of FrF 375,000 and the rates applicable to any gifts in excess of this abatement apply as follows:

| Band of Value | Rate of Tax % |
|---|---|
| Less than FrF 100,000 | 40 |
| FrF 100,000 upwards | 50 |

A couple in a PACS cannot enter into a community property contract so they cannot avail themselves of the most tax-efficient method of passing property from one spouse to another.

### 2.6.3 Ownership of French property via a company

Under Article 529 of the French Civil Code, a shareholder's interests in a company are classed as movable property and pass in accordance with the law of the country where he is habitually resident. A shareholder who remains domiciled or habitually resident in the UK can therefore dispose of his shares in a company during his lifetime or on death in accordance with English law, thereby postponing the rules of French succession law which would otherwise apply if the property were held directly by individuals *en indivision* or *en tontine*.

#### a) Offshore companies

Non-French resident individuals considering an investment in French property often ask whether they should form an 'offshore' (i.e. tax haven) company to own their new investment. The answer is usually in the negative for the following reasons:

● Transfers of property to tax-haven companies pay the full rate of stamp duty (currently nearly 20%).

● The French will assess the offshore company to a 3% tax per annum on the market value of the property it owns in France.

● In addition, the company will pay French corporation tax on any rental income it obtains from the property. The rate of corporation tax will normally be 33.33%, whereas an individual in receipt of rental income from France would be likely to suffer tax at the minimum rate for non-French residents which is currently 25%. The minimum corporation tax charge for companies with a turnover of between FrF 500,000 and FrF 1,000,000 is FrF 5,000. The property in France could be regarded as a permanent establishment of the foreign company, in which case it may have to register its presence in France and comply with various administrative filing requirements.

● An individual is entitled to indexation relief and to write off 5% of the gain for each year of ownership beyond the second. A company is entitled to neither of these reliefs.

● The shareholders who have the use of the French property would have a personal French income tax liability calculated either as a notional income of three times the rental value of the property if they reside in countries which do not have double tax treaties with France. If they live in treaty partner countries, their own country may seek to tax them on a benefit in kind (afforded to them in the form of the rent-free occupation of the property) basis.

● Commercial companies owning French property without letting it have been known to be taxed on a notional rental income under the *acte anormal de gestion* principle (ie abnormal management).

It is conceivable that in the case of a very valuable investment, the exposure of the non-resident to French gifts, inheritance and wealth tax could call for more sophisticated planning. In this situation, however, it will generally be much simpler to reduce the size of the French estate exposed to French capital taxes by borrowing to finance the acquisition of the property.

### b) Ownership of French property via an SCI

Ready-made 'off the shelf' companies do not exist in France. Companies are generally divided into those which have 'civil' objects and those which have 'commercial' objects. The test of commerciality is essentially the intention to buy and sell goods.

A *Notaire* will usually charge between FrF 10,500 and FrF 30,000 to incorporate and register a *Société Civile Immobilière* or civil property-holding company (the 'SCI'). Notwithstanding the costs of incorporating an SCI, there are many situations where it is desirable to use one, for example where more than one investor is involved, or where foreign investors wish to avoid the consequences of French succession law by holding only personal property in their own names.

For tax purposes, an SCI is deemed to have no existence distinct from its members and each shareholder is treated as an owner of the land. Income from unfurnished lettings is assessed on the individual shareholders and gains realised on a sale of the shares by an individual are subject to the private capital gains tax rules. A fiscally transparent company therefore allows advantage to be taken of the favourable tax treatment accorded to individuals, while using a corporate form. An SCI which lets its property out on a furnished basis is a special case, as described at 7.4. The use of an SCI is not however a universal panacea, and you should consider the burden of complying with company law and tax reporting requirements when exploring this option. It may also be difficult to raise loan finance from a French bank if a company is used.

### c) Other companies

For convenience many investors choose to use a company registered in their own home country. They understand the relevant company law and can carry on the administration themselves. Provided the country of their residence has a double tax treaty with France, and they comply with the French reporting requirements, such a company will not suffer the 3% annual tax on the market value of the French property. However, it is seldom possible to make a foreign company fiscally transparent in France. The company will therefore be subject to French corporation tax and the other disadvantages applicable to offshore companies.

### 2.6.4 Ownership via trusts

The concept of the trust does not exist in French law, and if property in France is owned by a trustee, the trustee will be treated (and taxed) as the full beneficial owner. It is therefore generally not wise for a trustee to acquire French real estate.

# 3. MAKING THE PROPERTY LETTABLE

The market for holiday lets in France is competitive and regular or return bookings are only likely if the property is well equipped and in a good structural condition.

## 3.1 RENOVATION AND CONVERSION

No 'development' (i.e. construction of a new house, a change to the outside aspect of an existing building such as replacement windows and doors, a new roof or an extension, or a change of use such as the conversion of a barn into residential quarters) should be undertaken on any property unless a *Certificat d'Urbanisme* ('CU') has been issued by the *Mairie* of the *commune* in which the property is situated confirming that your project can go ahead.

Generally speaking, planning permission (*permis de construire*) must also be obtained before any development or modernisation. Planning permission is not usually necessary for:

● fences no higher than 2 metres above ground;

● terraces no higher than 0.6 metres above ground;

● posts, aerials, etc no higher than 12 metres above ground;

● any work of less than 2 metres$^2$ in area and 1.5 metres above ground;

● statues or monuments no higher than 12 metres above ground or of no greater volume than 40 cubic metres.

Works carried out inside the property (such as bathroom or kitchen conversions) can, with certain exceptions, usually be carried out without planning permission provided they conform to local building regulations. Demolition work is often subject to planning permission, but work such as the maintenance of façades or the construction of an outdoor swimming pool can usually be undertaken without planning permission by obtaining an exemption certificate one month before the work is due to start. Depending on the region, the installation of septic tanks may also require planning permission.

French builders (*artisans*) are required to register with the local chamber of trade (*Chambre des Métiers*) and with the national standards institute (*OPQCB*) which issues certificates of competence. *Artisans* and other properly registered builders in France are required to carry insurance cover which underwrites the guarantees of the quality of their work and of its conformity with the codes of practice and building regulations.

To encourage the general upgrading of French properties, the VAT payable on renovation material and renovation work invoiced from 15 September 1999, has been reduced from 20.6% to 5.5% for a trial period of three years.

## 3.2 FURNITURE

Unless the property is in an area where the demand for high class-accommodation is great, furniture need not be luxurious but should be solid, comfortable and easy to maintain or clean.

Many tenants prefer separate bedrooms for the different members of their group. Double beds reduce the number of family permutations, and therefore the potential market, particularly when two or more families want to share the use of the property at the same time. Children will usually double up but relying on a sofa/folding bed for adults will not endear a property to the majority of tenants. The beds should have washable calico covers, and each bedroom should have a wardrobe. Recurrent complaints include the poor quality of beds and lack of easy chairs.

## 3.3 LINEN

Some landlords choose to provide linen, but it may be more trouble than it is worth, and it is not unreasonable to expect tenants to bring their own. If linen is provided tenants should be told in advance of any extra charge for cleaning sheets, towels and pillow cases at the local *blanchisserie*. It is also wise to keep a spare set of linen in case of any unexpected need. Duvets may be preferred to blankets, but this is a matter of personal choice. There should be two pillows for each bed.

## 3.4 KITCHEN EQUIPMENT

Poor cooking facilities are another source of complaint. There should be sufficient matching sets of crockery, cutlery, cooking utensils and other essential items which should be both durable and of reasonable quality. Tenants will not usually put up with cracked cups, burnt saucepans etc, and will expect everything provided in the kitchen and bathroom to be clean and functional.

## 3.5 DOMESTIC EQUIPMENT

The domestic equipment provided for the tenant's use should be in good working order and you should take out service contracts for washing machines, dish-washing machines, cooking and other appliances. Although heating is not particularly important during the summer months, some provision should be made in case of the odd cold evening, which is not unusual even during the warmest months. Efficient portable electric heaters may be the most appropriate method. If the property has central heating, the system should be turned off before each letting. The tenant can, of course, turn it on if he chooses. Whatever type of heating is provided, the power consumed should be metered and charged for. It is advisable to ensure that the central heating system is serviced regularly.

## 3.6 CLEANING, MAINTENANCE, CARETAKING AND RECEIVING GUESTS

A friendly neighbour or other dependable local catetaker should be retained to inspect the interior and generally keep an eye on the property throughout the year so that any problems (e.g. burst water pipes) can immediately be rectified. It is important that the property is refurbished before the start of the letting season and some annual maintenance and decoration is usually necessary.

The property should also be thoroughly cleaned before the start of each letting period.

A cold fridge stocked with basic groceries (e.g. eggs, butter and milk), hot water and a few flowers make tenants feel even more welcome.

## 3.7 INSURANCE AND SAFETY

It is an offence not to have minimum third party public liability insurance or *assurance à responsabilité civile* on completion of your purchase. Fire insurance cover is also obligatory. Your insurance cover should as a minimum be extended to include damage or injury to neighbours and third parties such as tenants or their guests (*recours des voisins et des tiers*). *Assurance multi-risques habitation* or householder's comprehensive insurance is an extension to the above cover which protects you not only against damage or injury to third parties but also usually covers:

● explosions, lightning and terrorist attacks;

● storms, hail and the weight of snow on roofs;

● natural disasters;

● damage to installations due to flooding or freezing;

● legal expenses;

● breakages;

● household accidents and damage to electrical appliances;

● theft and acts of vandalism.

Your insurance company should be notified that the property is being used for holiday lettings. You should also ensure that the policy is extended to cover damage caused to the property by the tenant or his guests, particularly fire and water damage. There should be no dangerous edges, traps or other hazards either inside or outside the property. Young children in particular should be considered when checking for hazards. If the property is near a road, there should be a fence or gate to prevent young children or animals running out. It is recommended that a first aid kit is provided, and put in an accessible place in the kitchen. The tenant should take out his own insurance to cover personal injury and theft or damage to his property.

The French authorities may refuse you permission to let on a commercial basis (see 6. below) if the property or its installations and equipment fail to comply with various standards, fire regulations and other safety laws. For example, all electrical wiring should be in good order and conform to the appropriate regulations and approved standards. If in doubt, a French electrical contractor should check this for you. Often, detailed plans are required, showing rooms with exit point fire doors, and an application fee will be payable. Your insurance company should be told that part of your property is to be let so that any necessary adjustments to the policy can be made.

# 4. MARKETING AND MANAGEMENT

The success or failure of your letting will very much depend on how well you market your property and manage the lettings. There is an enormous choice in where to advertise, so you should aim at the widest possible audience all year round. The Internet is a must because of the number of people who now have access. Various French laws penalise landlords who advertise in a misleading way (*publicité mensongère*) or misdescribe the true quality, quantity or fitness of the property and its equipment. There are criminal fines ranging from FrF 2,500 to FrF 5,000 for breaches of these laws and/or imprisonment for up to four years. An injured party may sue for damages if any have been suffered and French consumer organisations may also claim damages for *préjudice public* from the landlord.

## 4.1 BROCHURES

You should prepare a concise and informative brochure which should contain:

- An attractive description of the area, immediate location (with a map referring to places of interest) and a photograph or drawing of the property, highlighting attractive features such as its architecture, outlook, garden and garden furniture. Invest in decent literature and make sure that photographs are without shadows, leafless trees, grey skies, or clutter in the foreground. A sunny balcony or a secluded terrace could give you the edge over other properties;

- A description of the facilities and equipment (e.g. washing machine, telephone, swimming pool) and information detailing distances to the nearest shops, restaurants, post office and sporting facilities such as golf, fishing etc;

- Details of booking periods (e.g. Saturday to Saturday), and the arrangements for receiving visitors on their arrival and handing over the keys. One major concern people have when booking properties direct with owners is that they are afraid they will have no comeback if they have cause for complaint.

- Details of the rent you charge which should to some extent be dictated by what other people charge locally, but care should be taken to compare like with like. You should also take into account the value of the French Franc against Sterling and other foreign currencies in so far as possible.

## 4.2 WHERE TO ADVERTISE

Advertising can be expensive and is often a matter of trial and error. Among different ways of advertising the property you may consider the following:

- National newspapers. Although effective at filling high season availability, linage adverts in the classified sections of newspapers can be very expensive if you want more than a few weeks of letting.

- Local or regional newspapers. For one small property only, it may well be more cost-effective using regional newspapers in a selected area.

- Periodical magazines are well used by self-catering property owners. Some of these magazines, such as The Lady, have pages of advertisements for holiday lettings during the height of the booking period in February and March. The cost of advertising varies considerably. There is a very wide range of choice, but some of the more unusual publications often produce the best results with the least expense. Depending on your area, an advertisement aimed at a more specialised readership might yield a good response.

- The French Government Tourist Board's nationwide and regional publications are worth considering. They are well used and, depending upon your area, are often well produced and a cost-effective place to advertise. Other publications, such as *Gîtes de France* or Brittany Ferries Magazine specialise in certain types of property, such as farm cottages. The response rate to advertisements in these annuals varies enormously. Owners of several units, or expensive property, may do well to consider these annual publications, but please note that most publishers require full details sometimes as early as June for release in the following year.

- Foreign advertising is risky for the inexperienced. Some town councils in France produce an accommodation register. It is often worthwhile to have your property listed, provided the cost is not prohibitive. Outside the U.K., the Belgians, the Dutch and the Germans are most interested in self-catering holidays in France. Agencies in the U.S. are particularly keen to take French properties onto their books. To attract overseas visitors it is often found best to locate a local agent through the tourist board in the country in question. The English Tourist Board (ETB) in London can supply the address of the tourist authority in other countries. The ETB offices in Europe are particularly helpful. If advertising is placed overseas, it should ask that replies be sent to the local agent.

## 4.3  LETTING AND MANAGING AGENTS

It may be more convenient to engage a letting agency to market and manage your property. French agents must have your written authority (*mandat de gestion*) to let the property and will usually ask you to sign their own short standard-form. It is important that you have this document thoroughly vetted before signature to ensure that your rights and obligations and the duties of the letting agent are clearly defined. For example, some French letting agents retain deposit cheques or rent paid by tenants and do not pay them into their bank account until the end of the tenancy or return them if they are not needed. For various legal reasons, it is important that the *mandat* states that the letting agent will immediately bank any monies received by a tenant as soon as they are received.

A number of UK-based agencies specialise in letting French property, some of which offer a complete marketing and fully-insured management service. Others do not provide local service in France and on-site cleaning, maintenance etc is therefore your responsibility.

Most agents charge commission based on a percentage of the rent charged. The percentage may vary depending on the amount of administration they are asked to carry out on your behalf. If you instruct a French letting agent on a full management basis (to include finding tenants, collecting rent, attending to any complaints, paying accounts, dealing with repairs and carrying out inspections) he will usually charge 20% of the rental plus French VAT (currently 19.6%). The fees charged by a letting or managing agent are however deductible against rental income for tax purposes.

# 5.   LETTING AGREEMENTS

With few exceptions (see Appendix A), the rights and obligations of landlords (*bailleurs*) and of their tenants (*locataires* or *preneurs*) will be governed by French law. It is important that a written tailor-made letting agreement (*contrat de location*) containing all the appropriate clauses for your protection is prepared and signed by the parties before the tenant takes occupation of the property in France.

Many landlords agree to let their property in France to tenants on an informal verbal basis. The tenancy will then be governed by the French Civil Code which offers landlords limited protection in the event of a dispute with the tenant. Similar problems may arise if a tenancy is agreed by exchange of correspondence, or under a loosely-worded written agreement. In some cases, the landlord may be unable to repossess the property at the end of the letting period. French letting agents (*agents locataires*) often invite landlords to sign a standard-form letting agreement which may contain clauses to the landlord's disadvantage. Some of these contracts bear English translations, but many are misleading and unintelligible.

## 5.1   SHORT-TERM LETS OF FURNISHED PROPERTY

Most UK or other tenants will only want to rent your property for a short holiday. Under French law, a tenant or his family cannot remain in the property at the end of the letting period if, in accordance with Articles 1714 to 1762 of the French Civil Code, and other *arrêtés* or *décrets* (laws):

● They have a permanent home elsewhere. Always check the position before you allow a tenant to take occupation of your property.

● The property is adequately furnished and equipped. If you let unfurnished or inadequately furnished property (e.g. a flat which has no kitchen, table, wardrobe and/or no bed), your tenants may be able to remain there indefinitely. Cases which have gone to court in France seem to suggest that a property is adequately furnished if, as a minimum, it has a bed, table, chairs, wardrobe, refrigerator and kitchen equipment. A properly drafted letting agreement should therefore contain an inventory (*inventaire*) signed by the parties which details the furniture and equipment in the property.

● The letting period is temporary and does not overrun the 'official' holiday season (*la saison*) which varies from region to region. For example, you can let property on the Mediterranean coast in the summer months and also around Christmas time. Elsewhere, the French holiday season usually runs from June till early September, although the ski resorts have a winter and a summer season. Wherever the property is located, the tenant may be able to remain in indefinite occupation if the letting period exceeds three months (Article 1 of a law (*arrêté*) dated 8 January 1993).

- The property is only let for holiday purposes. The tenant should at no times be allowed to conduct any business or study in the property.

- The property should comply with the minimum requirements of *décret* 87-149 of 6 March 1987 which states, inter alia, that the property should be 'free of permanent noxious odours' and is 'situated away from areas likely to be a nuisance to holidaymakers' (e.g.major roads, railways and airports).

### 5.1.1 The landlord's main obligations

Whatever a letting agreement says, the French Civil Code states that a landlord must:

- Allow the tenant to enjoy quiet possession (*jouissance paisible*) of the property. The landlord is not, however, liable for acts of third parties which affect the tenant's rights of quiet possession (e.g. theft). The landlord may enter the property to carry out urgent structural alterations or repairs which cannot be put off until the end of the letting period;

- Ensure that the property and its equipment are in a good state of repair and fit for their intended use before the tenant takes possession, unless the tenant unreservedly accepts any imperfections which are brought to his attention before he takes occupation.

- Carry out all works necessary to keep the property and its equipment in a good state of repair whilst the tenant is in occupation.

### 5.1.2 The tenant's main obligations

Under the French Civil Code, a tenant must:

- Pay the agreed rent and charges in the manner prescribed by the landlord;

- Not use the property for any purposes other than those agreed;

- Not be a nuisance to neighbours and the general public during the letting period;

- Take care of the property and be responsible for any damage caused by his family and guests. If the property and/or its furniture and equipment are damaged or destroyed by fire, Article 1733 of the French Civil Code presumes the tenant to be responsible, whether or not caused deliberately or accidentally, unless the tenant can prove that the fire was caused by a structural defect, a third party, or by *force majeure*;

- Return the property to the landlord at the end of the letting period in the same state and condition as it was when he took possession.

If the tenant fails to comply with these obligations, the landlord can usually terminate the letting agreement with immediate effect and the tenant may be liable to pay the landlord rent for as long as it takes to make the property lettable again. This should be pointed out to the tenant before he takes occupation of the property.

## 5.2 CONTENTS OF A SHORT-TERM LETTING AGREEMENT

To protect the landlord against most foreseeable problems, a written letting agreement (see Appendix A) containing the following essential clauses should be signed and exchanged by the parties:

a) Full details of the landlord and tenants (name, address and telephone number).

b) A precise legal identification of the property (*description des lieux* or *état descriptif*) and those fixtures and fittings of which the tenant will have exclusive use (or use in common with others) during the letting period. Under a French law of 16 May 1967, a full description of the property should be supplied to and approved by the tenant before he takes up occupation. This description should detail which rooms are to be used as bedrooms; the kitchen and bathroom facilities available; parking facilities (if any) and distances to nearby facilities, e.g. the beach, ski slope, shops etc. The agreement should also state whether cutlery, linen, a telephone and/or television are provided, and whether they will be charged for separately.

c) The date and time when the letting period commences and ends, and to whom the tenant should return the keys. The tenancy will automatically be renewed if the tenant is expressly or tacitly allowed to remain in possession of the property at the end of the original letting period.

d) The amount of the rent (*loyer*). There are no legal limits on the amount of rent which can be charged for a short-term tenancy. As debt recovery procedures can be lengthy and expensive to pursue, the rent should preferably be paid in full before the tenant takes occupation of the property.

e) The amount of the deposit (*dépôt de garantie*) payable by the tenant which a prudent landlord should insist on receiving to cover the cost of repairing or replacing any damage or loss caused by the tenant or his guests to the property, its equipment or contents. An inventory of the contents should also be prepared, signed by the parties and annexed to the letting agreement before the tenant takes occupation and when he leaves. If the property and its contents are intact when the tenant leaves the property, he will recover his deposit in full. If (apart from fair wear and tear) any property damage has been done, or items listed in the inventory are broken, missing or have not been replaced, the letting agreement should state that the landlord can deduct the necessary repair or replacement costs from the deposit.

There are two types of deposit. One is called *arrhes* and the other *acompte*. If the tenant is in breach of contract, he loses his *arrhes*. He may be sued for damages as well. But if the landlord breaks the contract, he must under Article 1590 of the French Civil Code repay twice the *arrhes* to the tenant. However, if the deposit is called an *acompte* or *dépôt de garantie* and the tenant is in breach of contract, again it is lost and he risks a claim for damages. But the landlord in breach only has to pay back what he received – and is not under the immediate penalty of double repayment. He may well be faced with a legal action for breach of contract, but that costs money and takes time. It is therefore essential that **any** prepayment should be described on a receipt, invoice or letting agreement as a *dépôt de garantie* or an *acompte*.

f)  A schedule of condition (*état des lieux*) can also be agreed and signed by the parties before the tenant takes occupation. This can be prepared by a letting agent in France. In the absence of a schedule of condition, the French Civil Code provides that the tenant is presumed to have taken the property in a good state of repair, unless there is evidence to the contrary.

g)  The amount of any extra charges for the use or consumption of water, electricity, gas and telephone. Many landlords charge a fixed amount (*charge forfaitaire*) for the supply of services. In some areas, a local *taxe de séjour* (tourist tax) may also apply.

h)  A list of 'house rules' to avoid possible arguments or complaints about, for example, loud music, unwelcome pets or anything else which might prove disruptive to neighbours or the general public. The letting agreement should also allow the landlord or his agents to inspect the property at regular intervals to keep an eye on the tenants or carry out any urgent structural alterations or repairs, no matter what nuisance this causes the tenants or whether they are deprived of the use of all or part of the property. It is possible to insert a 'penalty clause' in the agreement, whereby a defaulting tenant is liable to pay a fixed sum penalty (which can be deducted from the deposit) if he fails to respect the house rules.

i)  If there are two or more tenants, the name of one tenant who will be personally liable for the rent, deposit and other charges, thereby enabling the landlord to sue that tenant for any losses if the other tenants refuse to pay or are in breach of the 'house rules'.

j)  A clause dealing with the assignment or sub-letting of the property. The letting agreement should provide that the landlord can immediately repossess the property and keep the deposit in full if the tenants allow friends or others who are not named in the letting agreement to take occupation of the property. It is an offence under French law to use or threaten force and harassment to gain entry into property, even when the occupants are there without the landlord's consent. A tenant who has been evicted in this way can also sue the landlord for damages and obtain a court order allowing him return to the property and remain in occupation for as long as he wishes.

k) A provision that the landlord is not responsible for loss or damage to the tenant's personal property.

## 5.3 LETTING FURNISHED PROPERTY FOR MORE THAN SIX MONTHS

Agreements to let furnished property in France for more than 6 months duration must be in writing and in the French language. A model form of letting agreement appears in Appendix A.3 which illustrates the terms and conditions which should be included. A prudent landlord should always have a letting agreement tailored to his requirements and approved by suitably qualified lawyers.

## 5.4 LETTING UNFURNISHED PROPERTY IN FRANCE

There is a large demand for long-term lets of unfurnished property in France which are governed by the Law of 6 July 1989 as amended by a Law of 21 July 1994. Although this type of letting is beyond the scope of this book, British landlords should be warned that their obligations are more onerous than if they let property on a furnished basis. The minimum letting period is usually three years if the landlord is a private individual (six years if a company). The landlord must give the tenant at least six months notice to quit the property and the grounds enabling him to repossess the property during the letting period are limited.

## 5.5 LETTING LAND

Do not allow farmers or anyone else the *usage agricole* (use for agricultural purposes such as pasture or cultivation) of your land in France in return for rent – no matter how small the payment – or other 'consideration' (e.g. a gift, or any produce he has farmed on your land) until you have checked your legal position carefully.

The farmer ('tenant') and his successors may otherwise be protected by strict French laws which, inter alia, entitle him to an agricultural tenancy (*bail rural*) over your land. If you ('landlord') wish to sell your property, the tenant has first rights to buy the freehold. If he does not want to buy, you can sell to a third party but the tenancy will continue, which may deter a potential buyer from proceeding.

French agricultural tenancies are often very informal and, although usually made in writing, can be created verbally. It is important that a formal tailor-made agreement containing all the clauses for your protection is prepared and signed by the parties **before** the tenant begins to use your land.

Whatever the terms of your agreement, French law states that the tenancy runs for a period of at least 9 years on payment of a specified (usually low) rent. The tenant can transfer the tenancy to his spouse or adult descendants. He or his successors can renew the tenancy for a further 9 years and so on every nine years. Unless the tenant agrees to terminate the agreement, the landlord can only repossess his land if the tenant fails to pay two rental payments; or engages in bad-husbandry (i.e. activities which adversely affect the proper running of the land); or fails to carry out any improvement recommended by the local *Commission Consultative*.

The landlord should declare any rental income received for French income tax purposes (see chapter 7). Where the income exceeds Frs 12,000 during the tax year (calendar year) on a property over 15 years old, the landlord may also suffer a tax on leases called *contribution autonome* (see section 7.3.3).

If you receive no payment or other 'consideration', none of the above legal or tax provisions applies. Similarly, no agricultural tenancy exists if you employ a gardener (or other non-farmer) to maintail land close to your buildings. Other exceptions include tenancies of woods, forests, small areas of land (depending on the *département*, usually limited to one or two hectares).

If you employ a gardener or other full/part time employee in France, the contract of employment must comply with the *Code du Travail* which limits the length of the working week and provides, inter alia, for a minimum wage, holiday entitle-ment and paid maternity leave. The procedure for dismissing an employee in France is very formalistic. You must also register with URSSAF, ASSEDIC and other bodies and pay French Social Security contributions which will represent about 40% of the employee's gross salary.

A friendly neighbour or other dependable local caretaker in France should be able to maintain the upkeep of your garden and land on an informal basis. If you feel that this can only be achieved by engaging the services of a local farmer, but do not want to grant an agricultural tenancy, a written *convention d'occupation précaire* (bare licence agreement) should be prepared by a qualified French lawyer. A properly drawn *convention* will avoid all of the potential legal and tax problems mentioned above.

# 6. LETTING AS A BUSINESS

There is good potential for profits if you buy:

● several residential properties;

● a large residential property for use by several different tenants at the same time;

● a *gîte*, bed and breakfast, *café*, bar, restaurant, hotel or other business (in some cases, a swimming pool, tennis court, bar, restaurant and other 'para-hotel' facilities such as a daily maid are also provided);

● a commercial property for occupation by tenants who intend to run their own business.

The procedure for buying or selling a commercial property in France is similar to that for residential property. However, to ensure that you set the business venture off on the right foot, you should be aware of the following points:

## 6.1 FRENCH TRANSFER DUTY

Under the French Commercial Code, a landlord is classified as a tradesman ('*commerçant*') and must register with the local *Chambre de Commerce* within two months of commencing trading if:

● the property is owned in the name of a commercial company (see 6.2.3 below); or

● the property is classed as commercial rather than residential or is residential in character but is run as a business. This will be the case if, for example, the property comprises or is intended to comprise more than 5 furnished self-contained rooms or units for let on a systematic basis. The meaning of the word 'systematic' does not necessarily mean that the unit or room must be let on a regular basis, but that it is available for let throughout the holiday season or for longer periods. Rooms and units which share the use of a kitchen, bathroom or other facilities and equipment may still be treated as being 'self-contained' for these purposes.

With effect from 1 January 1999, transfers of properties, which fall into one of the above categories, attract a transfer registration duty of 4.8% instead of the 18.2% rate applicable before then.

## 6.2 STRUCTURING THE INVESTMENT

Although in general terms it is simpler and cheaper to run a business in France as an individual or group of individuals, the transfer duty problem can be avoided by owning a commercial property (*les murs*) in France through the medium of a

French civil company (the 'SCI') provided that the SCI does not itself engage in commercial activities but delegates this task to a separate company.

This type of structure can not only help to secure the maximum tax advantage whilst retaining the benefit of limited liability against the commercial risks inherent in the business, but also circumvent the effects of French succession law. It is possible to use a UK or other non-French company structure but for tax reasons this option is rarely beneficial.

### 6.2.1 The property

Although you can either buy a residential or a commercial property (freehold or leasehold), it may be easier to buy an existing business in France than to create a new one. If you want to buy the freehold of the property and (if there is one) the existing business at the same time, there will usually be two separate contracts. If you do not have a large amount to invest, you may be able to purchase the *fonds de commerce* only and take a lease (*bail*) of the property from the landlord with an option to purchase the freehold from him at a later date.

Leases of business or commercial premises in France are governed by Law 53.960 of 30 September 1953. As a general rule, a business lease may not be for less than nine years. A business tenant generally has security of tenure and is entitled to compensation if his lease is not renewed in cases where the law so allows.

### 6.2.2 The business

If you buy an existing *fonds de commerce* the registration tax payable is a fixed charge of FrF 100 up to FrF 150,000 and a rate of 4.8% of the value exceeding FrF 150,000.

The *fonds de commerce* will often be owned and managed by a French limited liability 'commercial' company which pays rent to the SCI or other entity which owns the freehold or leasehold of the property. In many cases, the shareholders in the SCI and the commercial company will be owned by the same individuals. In addition to the advantages of setting up or buying into this type of structure, if the business does not work out, your property will remain in the ownership of the SCI, which will not necessarily be affected by the failure of the company which runs the business. You can sell the business, but keep the property, thereby drawing an income from the lease of the property to whoever purchases your business. The rent paid by the commercial company is deducted from its income or profits which are subject to French corporation tax. This structure is also an advantage for the new owner, as it reduces the amount of initial capital required by him to take over the business.

### 6.2.3 French commercial companies

There are two ways of carrying on a business in France. The first is as a sole trader (*entreprise individuelle*) and the second is through a corporate body (*société*).

Although an *entreprise individuelle* is the smallest form of business organisation and the simplest to run, it does not have the protection of limited liability. A sole trader is personally liable for all debts arising in connection with his business. By contrast, the liability of the members for the debts of a *société*, depending on its type, may or may not be limited.

In France, the first broad category of *société* corresponds to an English law partnership where the members have unlimited liability for the debts of the *société*. The second category corresponds approximately under English law to a limited liability company where the liability of members is usually limited to their investment in the capital of the company.

The two most popular forms of limited liability company structures in France are the SARL (*Société à Responsabilité Limitée*) and the SA (*Société Anonyme*). An SARL corresponds to an English private limited company. The SA is similar to an English public limited company in its structure and purpose.

One relative advantage of a SARL over an SA is that a SARL only requires two members with a total of FrF 50,000 in capital, whereas forming a SA requires seven shareholders to contribute a total of FrF 250,000. Moreover, an SA's balance sheet must be published publicly, but a SARL's can remain private.

One of the disadvantages of a SARL relative to the SA form is that shares in a SARL must be entirely paid-up at the time of incorporating the company. Only one-quarter of the nominal value of an SA's shares have to be paid-up when issued, the remainder can be payable over five years.

An SARL may not issue negotiable bonds. Consequently all financing must derive from bank loans and investment by members. The SA is the only limited liability company structure that can issue various types of negotiable securities and offer its shares to the public. It is therefore the appropriate form of business structure for operations whose capital requirements are large and cannot be satisfied by a restricted number of shareholders, or which need to offer negotiable shares and bonds to finance their growth.

The SA is usually considered to be more suitable to large scale operations in view of its more complicated management and control structure. The SARL is extensively used by businessmen who wish to use a limited liability vehicle without using the more complex form of an SA in the context of small to medium size operations.

Other forms of commercial company exist,in particular the société en nom collectif ('SNC') – a general partnership – and the société en commandite simple ('SCS') which is a limited partnership. The SCS has many tax and legal advantages when the management team, composed of individuals,is unable to put much equity into the company but wishes and deserves not only to have an efficient incentive by way of sharing in the profits but also to enjoy a certain independence vis a vis the shareholders (e.g. venture capitalists). The main problem of this form, ie the unlimited liability of the general partner, can easily be solved as a general partner can itself be a limited company (SA or SARL).

The SNC, which is not subject to French corporation tax, is often used within French industrial groups for subsidiaries contemplating losses which can, in this case, be deducted at parent level.

Since 1994 there has been a new form of company called a société par actions simplifiées which is a vehicle for joint ventures between very large corporations.

Whatever the form of company, the legal incorporation and publicity formalities involved take about 15 days after the execution of the by-laws and the payment of the share capital to be issued (100% for a SARL, 25% for a SA) into a special account opened with a bank where the money is kept in escrow until the delivery of the certificate of incorporation by the Registre du Commerce et des Sociétés.

By-laws and minutes of general meetings do not need to be executed in the presence of a Notaire. If the by-laws so permit, general meetings of shareholders and the meetings of the Board can be held outside France.

With the exception of dealing with the formalities relating to the remaining foreign exchange controls (which are about to be greatly reduced), French companies controlled by foreigners are treated in exactly the same way as other French companies.

## 6.3    RUNNING A BUSINESS IN FRANCE

As a *commerçant*, you should at least have a reasonable knowledge of spoken French in order to keep on top of the administration and comply with the various tax and other official documents you will receive each year, failing which you may face a hefty fine. The Chambre de Commerce may run a *stage de gestion* (management course) for the small business. In some cases, the course is compulsory. The local *Chambre des Métiers* may also, at reasonable cost, offer to help you deal with some or all of the paperwork involved in running the operation in France . Language barriers apart, the officers at the *Chambre de Commerce*, the tax office and other administrative authorities are usually very helpful.

### 6.3.1  Planning permission

Planning permission must usually be obtained before your property can be used or converted for use by members of the public. The application should be sent to the local *Mairie* who will consult with the public health, fire and other authorities before permission is granted. Permission may be refused if, for example, the property is unhygienic or does not comply with the provisions of *décret* No 73-1007 of 31 October 1973 which protects the public against risks of fire and panic.

### 6.3.2  Sale or supply of alcohol

The licensing of premises where alcohol and soft drinks are consumed is strictly regulated by the *Code des débits de boissons*. You cannot obtain a *licence* (licence) before completing a *déclaration préalable* (prior declaration) which must be filed with the *Mairie* (in some cases, the *Préfecture de Police*) at least 15 days before the opening date. A further declaration must also be made to the *recette locale des douanes et droits indirects* who are primarily responsible for French VAT and other indirect taxes. Applications are usually processed within a fortnight.

Proprietors of restaurants, hotels and *chambres d'hôtes* who serve drinks (even free of charge) with main meals and as accompaniments to food must hold a *licence restaurant*. A *petite licence* is required where only soft drinks, beers, wines and other alcohol with a content of less than 3% are provided. If spirits and other drinks with an alcohol content of up to 18% are also served, you must hold a *grande licence restaurant*. Hotel and restaurant licences can be obtained relatively easily with no limit on numbers.

It is harder to obtain a licence to serve alcohol and soft drinks if food is **not** served on the premises. The authorities cannot issue new licences in excess of the permitted number per *département* at any one time. Nor can you transfer an existing licence from premises in (say) Paris to Marseille. A *Licence I (boissons sans alcool)* permits the sale of soft drinks only. *Licence II (boissons fermentées)* holders can also sell wines, beers and other drinks with an alcohol content of less than 3%. A *Licence III (restreinte)* authorises the sale of the above and drinks with an alcohol content of no more than 18%. Finally, a *Licence IV (de plein exercice)* holder can sell all these drinks as well as spirits. In popular resorts, a *Licence IV* will be very expensive to buy. A proprietor who does not hold a valid *licence* or who is otherwise in breach of the *Code des débits de boissons* can face heavy fines and other civil or criminal penalties. In serious cases, premises can be closed for up to twelve months by order of the *administration*.

### 6.3.3 Restaurants and hotels

It is important to ensure that an alcohol licence is being sold with the business and no purchase commitment should be made until this point has been carefully checked. You may also want to prevent your vendor from opening a rival establishment within a certain radius of the property in which case this should be agreed in writing before you sign a contract.

Before you can open a restaurant or hotel in France to the public, the property must first be inspected by a number of administrative bodies and a licence obtained to ensure that the establishment complies with strict safety and hygiene standards. You must also register the business at the local *Chambre de Commerce*.

### 6.3.4 Employment law and social security

If you employ a cook, cleaner, gardener or other full/part time employee in France, the contract of employment must comply with the *Code du Travail* which limits the length of the working week and provides, inter alia, for a minimum wage, holiday entitlement and paid maternity leave. The procedure for dismissing an employee in France is very formalistic.

You must also register with 'URSSAF', 'ASSEDIC' and other bodies and pay Social Security contributions which will represent about 40% of the employee's gross salary.

# 7.   TAXATION

The tax year in France is the year to 31 December. The basic tax law in France is the *Code Général des Impôts* ('CGI') which is subject to frequent amendment, both by specific *lois fiscales* and the annual *loi de finances*.

A French resident taxpayer will normally deal with one of more than 800 *Centres des impôts*, appropriate to the place where he lives. Non-residents will normally deal with the *Centre des Impôts des Non-Résidents* at 9, rue d'Uzès, 75094 Paris Cedex 02.

A UK resident who lets out a property in France will have a UK liability to income tax computed under the Schedule A rules. He will be entitled to credit against his UK tax bill for the French tax which he has paid on his French rental income.

## 7.1   TAXATION OF RENTAL INCOME FROM FRENCH PROPERTIES OWNED BY NON-RESIDENTS

### 7.1.1   *Self declaration*

Income from letting French property must be declared to the French authorities by 30 April in each year, even if neither the owner or the tenant of the property reside in France. The onus is on the taxpayer (and not his letting or other agent) to complete and submit the returns which the law obliges him to make. A non-resident taxpayer can also be asked to designate a tax representative in France.

Whether intentionally or unintentionally, many UK and other non-resident landlords fail to declare their rental income to the French tax authorities. This lax attitude has to some extent been encouraged by the historic nonchalance of the French tax offices, although more recently French tax inspectors have been reviewing cadastral and other property records, letting agents' records and small advertisements in local French and foreign newspapers to trace undeclared lettings.

### 7.1.2   *Penalties for late payment or filing incorrect returns*

If a non-resident does not submit a return, the administration may send him a return with a *demande de déclaration* asking him to complete and submit it. The next step is that the administration sends a reminder to him (called a *mise en demeure*). If he then fails to regularise the position within 30 days, the administration can issue an estimated assessment (*taxation d'office*). The onus is then on the taxpayer to disprove the assessment. Interest on overdue tax is charged at 0.75% per month and there is a penalty of 10% if the taxpayer has made his return late but before he receives the *mise en demeure*, or if he responded within 30 days of receiving the *mise en demeure*. The penalty increases to 40% thereafter and to 80% if the taxpayer does not respond to a second *mise en demeure*.

The tax office can assess up to 3 years in arrears, and needless to say, this can give rise to heavy tax bills.

## 7.2    BASIS OF ASSESSMENT

### 7.2.1   *Residence*

If you are habitually resident in France, you are entitled to tax reductions for various home ownership expenses in respect of a principal residence, but these tax reductions are not normally available to non-residents. Your taxable rental income will be added to your general income and taxed according to the '*barème de l'impôt*' (income tax scale) after taking your family circumstances and charges into account.

Certain non-resident individuals who let their French property are subject to French income tax on a notional income (*base forfaitaire*) equal to three times the rental value of the property, unless their French rental income is greater. However this does not apply to individuals resident in the UK or residents of most of the other countries that have double tax treaties with France. The people concerned by this charge include residents of the Channel Islands, the Isle of Man, Andorra and Monaco.

An individual who is affected will have to pay the charge even if he does not let out the property or has the use of the property for only part of the year. If he lets the property, the rental value is that specified in his letting agreement or lease unless this appears artificially low. If he has more than one property in France, the charge is based on 3 times the total rental values of all the properties. The income so determined is the final taxable income, and the non-resident cannot claim to deduct any home ownership expenses or other charges (see below) against income, or any losses on rented properties. The only silver lining to this cloud is that the minimum income tax rate of 25% (see below) is not applied to non-residents assessed on this basis.

A UK or other resident individual in a French treaty partner country who owns residential property in France is protected from the notional income basis of assessment and will not normally have a liability to French income tax unless he lets the property out. He will be taxed at a minimum rate of 25% on his French rental income, but the taxable amount will vary depending on the elements described below. Losses can only be set against other rental income liable to income tax in France and can be carried forward for 5 years. UK residents can set French tax paid against tax levied in the UK in respect of their French rental income (see 7.6 below). However, if a UK resident owns the property through the medium of a company, it is possible that he may be assessed to tax on the benefit-in-kind of the rent-free use of the property.

### 7.2.2 Unfurnished property

If an unfurnished property is let commercially by an individual, either directly or through the medium of an SCI or other fiscally transparent company, the rental income is assessable under the *revenus fonciers* rules. The income is normally reported on forms 2042 and 2044 which then need to be submitted to the *Centre des Impôts des Non-Résidents* ('CINR') in Paris.

The expenses that may be deducted from gross rental income, as and when they are paid, are as follows:

- Local property tax, *taxes foncières* (tax on land and building). The tenant should normally pay the *taxe d'habitation* (occupier's rate) if he was occupying the property as at 1 January of the tax year. If the *taxe d'habitation* is paid by the landlord then the latter is entitled to recharge this cost to the tenant.

- *Contribution autonome* (tax on leases, see 7.3.3)

- repairs and maintenance;

- management expenses (*concierges*, *gérants* or *administrateurs d'immeubles*);

- improvements (such as the cost of installing central heating, lifts, telephones etc);

- interest on all debts incurred in the acquisition, construction, repair or improvement of the property, and also interest on debts incurred to preserve the owner's title to the property (e.g. interest on a loan taken out to pay inheritance tax on the property). There is no limit on the amount of interest that is deductible or to the period of time during which the interest on the loan may be deducted. The costs of borrowing (e.g. bank facility fees) are equally deductible. If the interest is incurred in the course of constructing a property and before the property is let, it can be offset against rental income from other properties let by the taxpayer, or it can be carried forward as a loss against future rental income;

- premiums for insurance against unpaid rent and any expenses that should have been (but were not) paid by the tenants and were met by the landlord;

- a *forfait* deduction of (currently) 14% of gross rental income (or 25% of rental income for shareholders in a *société civile de placement immobilier*) to cover management expenses not covered above such as telephone, travel, correspondence, house insurance, accounting, legal and tax advice, and letting agents fees.

When claiming such deductions one must ensure that evidence of all expenses incurred is available for further checking. In addition, where rural property is let, it is accepted that the 14% *forfait* deduction does not cover the cost of insurance, and the actual cost may be claimed, along with the cost of improvements to barns and other installations which are not habitable.

Losses on the letting of unfurnished property may be carried forward for up to ten years.

Instead of itemising his expenses, a landlord whose rental income from unfurnished lettings does not exceed FrF 60,000, can elect to be taxed under the *Micro-Foncier* regime, which means that 40% of the gross rent is deducted as representing the total amount of expenses related to the rental income. The FrF 60,000 limit applies to the income for a whole year, and is adjusted pro rata temporis if the letting activity only takes place during part of the year. This option is not available to landlords who benefit from other tax advantages, such as owners of historic monuments and landlords who benefit from accelerated depreciation allowances. The election for the *Micro-Foncier* regime covers a three-year period, and is irrevocable during that time.

### 7.2.3 Furnished property

If a property is let furnished by an individual on an habitual basis, the income is normally assessed under the rules for business income (*bénéfices industriels et commerciaux*). However, if the accommodation let is part of the principal residence of the landlord:

● the income is totally exempt if the accommodation constitutes the principal residence of the tenant; and

● if it does not constitute the principal residence of the tenant, income of up to FrF 5,000 is exempt (e.g. for the letting of guest rooms and *chambres d'hôtes*).

Under the business income rules, the assessable income will be determined on a forfeit basis, a simplified real basis or the normal basis depending on the annual turnover and the tax status of the landlord. For individuals, the taxable income will be calculated on one of the following bases:

i)   *Micro BIC*

If the rental receipts are currently less than FrF 500,000, and the letting is considered as a non-professional activity, the taxpayer will normally be assessed on the *Micro BIC* regime. Only 30% of the gross rental income is subject to taxation, since 70% is deducted to cover all charges and expenses of the letting. At first glance this method seems generous, but the result is always a profit even when the activity in fact generates losses.

ii) *Régimes réels*

The *Régime réel normal* or *Régime réel simplifié* methods of taxation – under which the actual expenses are estimated or calculated – is sometimes more advantageous. If the rental receipts are above FrF 500,000 but below FrF 5 million (excluding VAT), the income will be calculated under the *réel simplifié* regime. If the rental receipts are over FrF 5 million, the income must be calculated on the *réel normal* basis.

The difference between the *réel simplifié* basis and the *réel normal* basis of calculating income lies primarily in the level of formality to be observed in the accounting. As a non-resident, the *réel* regimes involve correspondence with both the local tax office and the tax office in Paris. The election for one or other taxation method must be made to the tax office before 1 February of the year for which the new method would be applicable. In other words, an option filed on 1 February 2001 would apply to income arising during 2001. Businesses subject to the *réel simplifié* regime prepare accounts (for VAT purposes and eventually for income tax purposes) on a quarterly basis.

The expenses that may be deducted when taxable income is calculated on a *réel simplifié* or *réel normal* basis are listed below.

Companies are excluded from the *Micro BIC* regime and therefore calculate their income under one of the *réel* regimes. If the property is let by a company subject to French corporation tax (see below), the basis period is the accounting year ended in the tax year and accounts are prepared on an accruals basis.

## 7.2.4 Deductible expenses

Where the property is treated as a business asset (see below), the expenses relevant to property income that are deductible under the *réel* regimes are:

● The general expenses of the business. These do not include expenses which are required to be capitalized, for example the costs associated with acquiring a property or architects' fees. Such payments are added to the cost of the property and may be depreciated. However, Notarial fees, registration taxes and estate agents fees are treated as expenses. The general costs of the business include interest and bank charges paid or payable, the costs of insurance and the costs of repairs and maintenance.

● Depreciation, which on residential housing is 1 to 2% of the cost of the property on a straight line basis.

● Provisions, for example, for doubtful debts and *taxes foncières* payable. Provisions for the expenses of construction or reconstruction or fitting out a property are not allowable.

However, if the property is put at the disposal of directors or shareholders for less than a market rent, the expenses relating to the period when the directors or shareholders occupy the property are not deductible.

### 7.2.5 Business asset

When declaring income from a furnished property, the taxpayer must decide whether the property will be treated as a business or personal asset as this will affect the tax computation.

An individual whose rental income is less than FrF 150,000 is normally classed as a 'non-professional landlord'. This means that he cannot deduct any losses on his rental activity from his other income (the losses can be carried forward for 5 years against future rental income) and any capital gain realised on a disposal of the property is taxed under the private capital gains tax rules.

If the taxpayer is registered at the local *registre de commerce* and either the rental income constitutes more than 50% of his total income or his rental receipts exceed FrF150,000, he is classed as a professional landlord. This means that he can offset any losses on his rental activity against his total income and any gain resulting from the sale of the property will be taxed as a business capital gain.

It should be borne in mind that the capital gains of a fiscally transparent company engaged in letting furnished property are exempt from capital gains tax if its turnover is less than FrF 1 million.

### 7.2.6 Choosing the right basis of assessment

Needless to say, one needs to compare all the options as the resulting tax bill may vary significantly. The options also need to be chosen very carefully as they can hide some pitfalls. For instance, if your annual rental income is below FrF 500,000, you are by law, assessable under the *Micro BIC* regime. However, you may opt for the *régime réel*, provided you apply before 1 February of the tax year for which the option is made. The option is usually irreversible.

Where your property is registered as a business asset, and if your rental income currently exceeds FrF 150,000, you will automatically be regarded as a professional landlord. If you should later wish your property to be treated as a personal asset, this reclassification will give rise to professional capital gains taxes as such a transfer is treated like a sale. Bearing in mind that the limit of FrF 150,000 (annual rents received) takes into account the notional income reported for your personal use of the property, it is quite easy to overstep this limit.

There would be no capital gains tax charge on reclassification of the property from the business asset to the personal assets category where annual rental income does not exceed the FrF 150,000 limit, as the landlord is then considered as a non-professional. Transfers at no value under this status do not therefore qualify as a sale.

## 7.3    OTHER FRENCH TAXES

French income tax is not the only tax applicable to French rental income. Lettings of furnished or unfurnished properties are liable, in some cases, to French VAT ('TVA'), business tax (*taxe professionnelle*) and, if the annual rental income from the letting exceeds FrF 12,000, a tax called *contribution autonome* is also payable.

### 7.3.1    *TVA*

The letting of furnished property is subject to TVA if the receipts of the taxpayer currently exceed FrF 500,000 and the property is a:

- registered tourist hotel and bed and breakfast lodging;

- registered tourist residence on a nine-year lease to a business which advertises abroad;

- Quasi – hotel business which provides, in addition to accomodation, hotel - like services (meals, cleaning, reception etc);

- property let (furnished or unfurnished) under a commercial lease to a busiess engaged in one of the activities described above.

Any lettings which do not match one of these categories are exempt from TVA.

When subject to TVA, the supply of furnished premises is charged at the reduced rate of 5.5%. However, the supply of food, telephone and other services is subject to TVA at the standard rate of 19.6%.

### 7.3.2    *Taxe professionnelle*

The business tax is due on most types of rental income with the exception of:

- one off 'incidental' lettings;

- the letting of part of one's principal residence, even on a regular basis, provided the price is reasonable;

- the letting of a property classified as a *Gîte de France* or *Meublé de Tourisme*;

- any other lettings of property which are used by the owner outside the letting season.

Although the exemption is a statutory right, provided the conditions listed above are fulfilled, it can be contested by any one of the local authorities (*Commune*, *Département* or *Région*).

### 7.3.3  Tax on leases

This tax applies on rental income, which is not subject to VAT. It includes any income received for the letting of fishing or hunting rights as well as furnished or unfurnished lets.

Known as the *droit de bail et contribution additionnelle* up to 1999, and then *contribution représentative du droit de bail* (CRDB) *et contribution additionnelle à la contribution représentative du droit de bail* (CACRDB), the tax on leases has undergone a number of changes in recent years. In a nutshell the CRDB applies to all 2000 lettings if the 1999 annual turnover was in excess of FrF 36,000 (FrF 12,000 prior to that date). A further charge, the CACRDB, applied if the property was over 15 years old and the rental income exceeded FrF 12,000. The rate was 2.5% for both taxes and calculated on the following taxable amount:

– the total rents received during the calendar year, plus

– any expenses normally payable by the landlord but paid by the tenants, less

– expenses paid by the landlord for the tenant (gas, electricity, water, and so on).

The landlord was able to recover the CRDB from his tenants and in the case of long-term lets this was the normal practice. The CACRDB charge was always met by the landlord.

The CRDB is suppressed with effect from 1 January 2001. However, the CACRDB remains in existence for the letting of properties over 15 years old if the rental income exceeds FrF 12,000. The name of the tax will be changed to *contribution autonome*, but the taxable basis and the rate will remain the same.

## 7.4  FRENCH CORPORATION TAX

French corporation tax (*impôt sur les sociétés*) is not a tax on French companies. It is a tax on the income of certain types of companies carrying on business in France. It does not apply to French companies carrying on business outside France or to French companies which are not 'capital' companies (e.g. SCIs). But it does apply to foreign 'capital' companies carrying on business in France.

Foreign capital companies are subject to French corporation tax on the profits of any business carried on in France. This is a very different basis from that which applies for income tax. There are three bases on which a French or foreign capital company can be said to be carrying on a business in France:

● it has a permanent establishment in France;

- it has a dependent agent in France;

- it habitually carries out a complete commercial cycle in France (e.g. purchase and sale).

Under many French double income tax treaties, a company is exempt from French corporation tax in respect of the profits of a trade or business if it is a resident of the treaty partner country and does not trade in France through a permanent establishment.

It is important to note that a French civil company (an 'SCI' – see 2.6.3(b) and 6.2) which rents out **furnished** accommodation is subjected to French corporation tax if its receipts from this activity constitute more than 10% of its turnover. This treatment arises because the letting of **furnished** accommodation is considered to be a commercial activity. A French SCI with UK resident shareholders and directors may well be regarded as resident in the UK, both under UK domestic law and under the provisions of Article 3 of the France-UK Income Tax Treaty. In this case the company will be liable to corporation tax in the UK, with credit for the French corporation tax suffered on its income.

These concepts are complicated and expert advice should always be sought before structuring your ownership of French property and/or the letting business through the vehicle of a French or foreign company.

## 7.5 TAXATION OF PROPERTY SPECULATORS

Profits realised by persons who trade in land (*marchands de biens*), profits of buying land with the intention of selling it after breaking it up into lots (*lotissements*) and profits of building (*profits de construction*) are calculated according to the business income rules and subject to income tax or corporation tax depending on the taxpayer. Building profits but must be calculated according to the *réel normal* or *réel simplifié* regimes (see 7.2.3). The question of whether a taxpayer is trading is essentially one of fact. Habitual operations carried out with a speculative intention are trading. With companies, the objects of the company and the business activities of the shareholders are taken into account.

Non-residents who engage in the activities described above are subject to a withholding tax of 50% on their profits.

## 7.6 LIABILITY TO TAX IN THE UK

Having properly declared and paid your taxes in France, you must then declare your rental income to the UK Inland Revenue. You can claim a credit for any French tax paid and you will only be taxed again to the extent that your liability to UK income tax exceeds the rate at which you were charged in France. So, if you are a higher rate taxpayer in the UK but have only been charged the minimum rate (25%) in France, you will be required to pay the difference to the Inland Revenue. Conversely, if you were charged a higher rate in France than your UK liability you will not be able to claim a refund for the difference.

Until the 1995 Finance Act came into force, the UK Revenue were notoriously reluctant to accept that the letting of a holiday home in France qualified as a business for UK tax purposes. They therefore generally denied relief against UK tax for any interest on money borrowed to acquire the property. Section 41 of the Finance Act changes the whole basis of the taxation of rental income from overseas properties. Although this source of income will still be assessed under Schedule D Case V, virtually all lettings of property in France will constitute part of a single 'Schedule A business', so that income on one property can be relieved against losses on another. Interest relief is available on the same basis as any other business expense, so that relief is available for interest on loans taken out to repair a French property or in respect of a vacant property (provided the property was acquired for the purposes of the business).

# APPENDIX A: PRECEDENTS

## PREFACE

The following precedents have been included as a guide only. Expert advice should always be obtained before completing any letting agreement.

### a) Language

Most of the precedents appearing below are in French. Superficially, it is interesting to see English language translations of French legal documents but there is little merit in providing these in a book of this nature. Literal translations usually make nonsense reading. On the other hand, to provide translations in wholly 'correct' English legal phraseology implies that the French law attached to the wording used in the original language is the same as attaches to the English translation. For example, it is not safe to translate the technical terms relating to repairs in a French lease by the use of phrases so commonly found in repairing covenants in English leases.

All French documents, of whatever kind, should be initialled by all the parties on each page as well as being signed on the last page. There is no need to have witnesses.

Strictly speaking, every translation from English into French for official use, i.e. by a *Notaire*, a Court or a local Companies Registry should be made by a *traducteur juré* or assermenté (sworn translator) in France, the cost of which can be very high and the end product not always wholly accurate. In certain cases, it can be well worthwhile approaching a suitable Notary Public in the UK whose translations are accurate and acceptable in France.

A Glossary will be found in Appendix C. It has been prepared for the reader who is not familiar with French legal phraseology and to avoid the need to resort to continuous translations and explanations in the text itself.

### b) Jurisdiction

Under Article 16 (1) of the 1968 Brussels Convention, most disputes concerning tenancies of French property concluded for temporary private use for a maximum period of six consecutive months can be subject to the jurisdiction of the Courts of England and Wales if:

a) The landlord and the tenant are both natural persons (i.e. neither is a company);

b) The landlord and the tenant are both domiciled in England and Wales.

In every other case, the letting agreement must always be subject to the jurisdiction of the French courts and must be written in the French language (see A.2 below).

If (English) tenants refuse to leave the property at the end of the letting period, the matter must always be dealt with by the French courts, whatever the letting agreement says.

c) **Law**

The tenancy will normally be governed by French law. It is possible for the parties to choose the law governing the contract, but the choice will be of limited effect as the mandatory requirements that the law of the country where the property is situated (France) will always apply irrespective of choice of law.

## A.1 ENGLISH-LANGUAGE AGREEMENT MADE SUBJECT MAINLY TO THE JURISDICTION OF THE COURTS OF ENGLAND AND WALES

### Agreement

BETWEEN

..................................................... (the 'Landlord' or the Landlord's agents appointed for the purposes of managing the property in the absence of the Landlord)

AND

..................................................... (the 'Tenant')

IT IS HEREBY AGREED AS FOLLOWS:

1. In this Agreement the following terms have the following meanings:

    1.1  'The Property' means .................................................................................

    1.2  'The Contents' means the fixtures and fittings, furnishings, furniture and effects in the Property which are specified in the attached Inventory signed by both parties.

    1.3  'The Term' means the term of ........................................ days/weeks/months.

    1.4  'The Commencement Date' means the ................. day of ................. 19........

    at ................. Hrs (local French time)

1.5 'The Termination Date' means the .................. day of .................. 19........

at .................. Hrs (local French time)

1.6 'The Rent' means £..................

1.7 'The Deposit' means a deposit of £.................. payable to the Landlord in accordance with clause 6. below. The Deposit paid does not constitute arrhes or a dédit and the parties waive the provisions of Article 1590 of the French Civil Code

2. The Landlord agrees to let and the Tenant agrees to take the Property together with the Contents for the Term commencing on the Commencement Date and terminating on the Termination Date at the Rent to be paid, of which £.................. is to be paid on the date hereof and the balance of £.................. is to be paid not less than ... weeks before The Commencement Date

3. The tenant hereby covenants:

3.1 To pay the Rent on the days and in the manner aforesaid

3.2 To pay and indemnify the Landlord against all rates and assessments of an annual and for all water, gas and electricity consumed or supplied to the Property and all charges for the use of the telephone (if any) at the Property during the Term and any permitted continuation thereof or a proper proportion of the amount of any such charges to be assessed according to the duration of the Term

3.3 To keep:

3.3.1 the interior of the Property clean and tidy (including but not limited to the painting, decoration and papering thereof) and

3.3.2 all those parts of the Property in as good and tenantable state of repair and condition as at the beginning of the Term reasonable wear and tear and damage by fire excepted

3.4 To use the Property in a Tenant-like manner

3.5 To keep the Contents clean, in good repair and condition and maintain all electrical and mechanical equipment in good working order (reasonable wear and tear and damage by fire excepted) and replace immediately any broken windows at the Property and from time to time replace any of the Contents which may be broken, lost, destroyed or so damaged by the Tenant, his family, servants or agents as to be unusable with others of similar value and appearance

3.6 Not to cause or suffer any damage or injury to be done to the Property by the Tenant, his family, servants or agents

3.7 To notify the Landlord forthwith in writing (except in the case of emergency) of any defect in the Property other than such as the tenant is liable to remedy under Clause 3.3 above as soon as practical after such defect comes to the notice of the Tenant

3.8 To permit the Landlord or his agents at reasonable hours in the daytime by appointment (except in the case of an emergency) to enter the Property to view their state and condition and that of the Contents, to take inventories and to execute repairs and other necessary works upon the Property or any part of the building of which the Property forms part, or any adjoining or adjacent building, and permit the Landlord or his agents to give notice to the Tenant of all dilapidations, wants of repair, cleansing, painting, restoration to the interior of the Property then found and of all such breakage, loss, destruction or damage of or to the Contents, as the Tenant shall be bound to make good then found and by such notice to require the Tenant to repair, cleanse, paint, restore or make good the same within .......... days/weeks from the service of such notice and if the Tenant fails by himself, his servants or agents to execute the said work within the said period permit the Landlord to enter upon the Property to execute the said work at the tenants expense

3.9 Not to make any alteration or addition to the Property or to paint, decorate or paper any part of the Property without first obtaining the Landlord's written consent to either the alterations or additions or the colour schemes for the painting, decoration and papering of the Property

3.10 To clean both sides of all windows at the Property as often as may be necessary

3.11 Not to remove, permit, cause or suffer to be removed any of the Contents from the Property or from the respective positions in the Property which they occupy at the commencement of the Term

3.12 Not at any time to bring onto the Property or any part a waterbed of any description whatsoever nor permit or cause or suffer any heavy objects to be brought onto the Property or any part thereof

3.13 Not to carry on, permit, cause or suffer to be carried on any trade, profession or study upon the Property nor receive paying guests but to use the Property only as a single private residence

3.14 Not to exhibit, permit, cause or suffer to be exhibited any poster or notice so as to be visible from the exterior of the Property

3.15 Not to permit, cause or suffer to be done on the Property anything which may be or become a nuisance or annoyance to the Landlord or the occupiers of any adjoining premises or which may render the Landlord's insurance of the Property void or voidable or increase the rate of premium for such insurance

3.16 Not to use, permit, cause or suffer the Property to be used for any illegal or immoral purpose

3.17 Not to make any noise or play any radio or television set or hi-fi or other music system or musical instrument in or about the Property between 23.00 hours and 07.00 hours so as to be audible outside the Property nor permit, cause or suffer the same

3.18 Not to block or cause any blockage to the drains, pipes, gutters, channels in or about the Property

3.19 Not to assign, sublet, share or part with possession or cease to occupy the whole or any part of the Property

3.20 Not to sell, charge or share possession of the Contents whether collectively or individually

3.21 Not to keep, permit or suffer to be kept at the Property or any part thereof without the Landlord's prior written consent any animal whether of a domestic nature or otherwise

3.22 To permit the Landlord or his agents at reasonable hours by appointment to enter the Property at any time during the Term with prospective tenants or purchasers of the Landlord's interest in the Property

3.23 At the Termination Date:

3.23.1 To yield up the Property and Contents any any articles substituted for the same in such state of repair and condition as shall be in accordance with the Tenant's obligations under this agreement

3.23.2 To pay for the washing (including ironing and pressing) of all linen, counterpanes, blankets etc (if any) and for the cleaning of all curtains which have been soiled during the Term

3.23.3 To make good or pay for the repair or replacements of such of the Contents as have been broken, lost or damaged during the Term or any continuation thereof (reasonable wear and tear and any damage by fire excepted)

3.24 To pay the costs of and incidental to the grant of this Agreement

3.25 Not by himself, his family, servant or agents to lop, top, cut down, remove or otherwise injure any trees, shrubs or plants growing at the Property or alter the general character of the garden but to keep the garden clean, tidy and in a proper state of cultivation according to the season of the year

4. The Landlord covenants that he will:

4.1 Permit the Tenant so long as he pays the rent and performs his obligations under this Agreement quietly to use and enjoy the Property during the Term without any interruption from the Landlord or any person rightfully claiming under or in trust for the Landlord

4.2 Keep in repair the structure and exterior of the Property (including the drains, gutters and external pipes) and insured against damage by fire

4.3 Keep in repair and proper working order the installations in the Property

4.3.1 for the supply of water, gas and electricity and for sanitation (including basins, sinks, baths and sanitary conveniences but not the fixtures and appliances for making use of the supply of water, gas or electricity) and

4.3.2 for space heating or heating water

4.4 This term shall not be construed as requiring the Landlord

4.4.1 to carry out any works or repairs for which the Tenant is liable by virtue of his duty to use the Property in a tenant-like manner

4.4.2 to rebuild or reinstate the Property in the case of destruction or damage by fire or by tempest, flood or other inevitable accident

4.4.3 to keep in repair or maintain anything which the Tenant is entitled to remove from the Property

4.5 In determining the standard of repair required by this Agreement regard shall be had to the age, character and prospective life of the Property and locality in which it is situated

4.6 Return to the Tenant any Rent payable for any period during which the Property may have been rendered uninhabitable by fire or any other risk against which the Landlord has insured

5. PROVIDED ALWAYS that, if at any time during the Term the Tenant fails to observe any of the stipulations in clause 3 hereof the Landlord may at any time thereafter re-enter upon the Property or any part thereof in the name of the whole and thereupon the tenancy granted shall absolutely determine but without prejudice to any claim of the Landlord in respect of any breach of the stipulations contained in clause 3 hereof

5.1 The Landlord acknowledges receipt from the Tenant of the Deposit on account of the Tenants obligations under clause 3 hereof which may be applied by the Landlord towards the cost of carrying out any works to the Property and/or for damage or breakage or repair to any of the Contents whether during the Term or at the Date of Termination

5.2 The Landlord agrees to repay the same to the Tenant within four weeks of the Date of Termination without interest after the deduction for any sums specified in clause 6.1

6. For the avoidance of doubt the Tenant is responsible for insuring his own contents and personal effects kept in the Property for the duration of this Agreement

7. IT IS AGREED AND DECLARED

7.1 That repossession proceedings and other matters directly affecting the Property shall be governed by French law and shall be subject to the exclusive jurisdiction of the French courts. All other matters concerning compliance with this Agreement shall be governed by English law and shall be submitted to the exclusive jurisdiction of the courts of England and Wales.

7.2 That prior to the execution of this Agreement the Tenant has read and approved the contents of this Agreement

Signed by the Landlord . . . . . . . . . . . . . . . . . . . . . . . . . . . . . . . . . . . . . . . . . . . . . . . . . . . . . . . . . . . .

Address . . . . . . . . . . . . . . . . . . . . . . . . . . . . . . . . . . . . . . . . . . . . . . . . . . . . . . . . . . . . . . . . . . . . . . . .

Occupation . . . . . . . . . . . . . . . . . . . . . . . . . . . . . . . . . . . . . . . . . . . . . . . . . . . . . . . . . . . . . . . . . . . . .

Signed by the Tenant .......................................................

Address ..................................................................

Occupation ..............................................................

Appendix

a) Inventory

b) Schedule of condition

c) Lease of the common parts (if applicable)

**A.2** **FRENCH LANGUAGE HOLIDAY LETTING AGREEMENT MADE SUBJECT TO THE JURISDICTION OF THE FRENCH COURTS AND TO FRENCH LAW**

*Engagement de Location Meublée Saisonnière*

Entre les soussignés: ........................................................

dénommé(s) 'Le bailleur' en singulier

Mandataire (le cas échéant):

et   ....................................................................

dénommé(s) 'Le locataire' en singulier

Le bailleur et le locataire ont convenu et arrêté ce qui suit:

Le bailleur loue au locataire qui accepte, à titre de location saisonnière, les locaux meublés ci-après désignés

1. Désignation des locaux

   Adresse: ...........................................................

   Type de logement: Appartement/Bungalow/Villa/Chalet/Maison individuelle

   Surface: ........................... m$^2$

   Nombre de pièces:

   tel que désigné dans l'état descriptif remis avant la rédaction de la présente location au locataire qui le reconnaît, et dont un exemplaire est annexé au contrat.

2. Conditions particulières

La présente location est consentie aux conditions générales figurant au Paragraphe 3, ainsi qu'aux conditions définies ci-après.

2.1 Durée

La présente location est consentie pour une durée de: ...............

Entrée: le ............. à ............. h ............. Sortie: le ............. à ............. h .............

2.2 Loyer TTC (cf 3.5)

|  | Sommes en toutes lettres | Sommes en chiffres |
|---|---|---|
| Loyer: | .................... F | .................... F |
| Charges: | .................... F | .................... F |
| Taxes: | .................... F | .................... F |

2.3 Taxe de séjour

|  | .................... F | .................... F |
|---|---|---|

(par personne et par jour)

2.4 Réservation (cf 3.3 et 3.4)

(a) Locaux classés:

Arrhes .................... F .................... F

(b) Locaux non classés:

.................... F .................... F

Arrhes ou acompte

2.5 Nettoyage: .................... F .................... F

2.6    Honoraires: (le cas échéant)

_____ . . . . . . . . . . . . . . . . . . . . F    . . . . . . . . . . . . . . . . . . . . F

Les honoraires sont à la charge du

Honoraires de location: _____ . . . . . . . . . . . . . . . . . . . . F

Frais d'état des lieux et d'inventaire: _____ . . . . . . . . . . . . . . . . . . . . F

Frais de dossier: _____ . . . . . . . . . . . . . . . . . . . . F

Total: _____ . . . . . . . . . . . . . . . . . . . . F

2.7    Documents annexés:

(a)    Etat des lieux contradictoire

(b)    Etat descriptif détaillé du logement

(c)    Inventaire du mobilier

(d)    En cas de location classée: Tableau de classement des locations

2.8    Couchage: Le couchage est prévu pour un nombre maximum de personnes fixé à: . . . . . . . . . . . . . . . . . . . . . . . . . . . . . . . . . . . . . . . . . . . . . . . . . . . . . . . . .

2.9    Dispositions complémentaires:

2.10   Remise des clés: Personne à contacter: M . . . . . . . . . . . . . . . . . . . . . . . . . . . . .

3. Conditions générales

3.1    Régime juridique du contrat

La présente location est conclue à titre de résidence provisoire et de plaisance.

Les locaux ne pourront être utilisés à titre d'habitation principale ou même secondaire et le locataire ne pourra y pratiquer aucune activité commerciale, artisanale ou professionnelle.

En conséquence, le contrat sera régi par les dispositions du Code Civil ainsi que par les conditions prévues aux présentes. En cas de contestation, compétence exclusive est attribuée aux Tribunaux Français.

3.2    Durée

Le bail cesse de plein droit à l'expiration du terme fixé (cf 2.1), sans qu'il soit nécessaire de donner congé. La location ne pourra être prorogée sans l'accord préalable et écrit du bailleur.

3.3    Formation du contrat

(a)    Réservation par le locataire

Le locataire effectuant une réservation signe et renvoie au bailleur le contrat accompagné IMPERATIVEMENT du montant de la réservation indiqué au 2.4.

Le solde de la location reste payable à la remise des clefs DES L'ARRIVEE.

(b)    Confirmation par le bailleur ou son mandataire

Dans un délai de 10 jours à compter de la réception du chèque de réservation, le bailleur ou son mandataire fait un courrier:

● soit confirmant au locataire la disponibilité des locaux, l'engagement des parties devenant ferme;

● soit restituant au locataire intégralement la somme versée, les locaux choisis par le locataire n'étant plus disponibles pour la période souhaitée.

Sur demande expresse du locataire, le bailleur ou son mandataire pourra conserver cette somme pour la location d'un local similaire ou pour une autre période, les conditions de cette nouvelle location étant immédiatement transmises au locataire en vue de recueillir son accord exprès.

(c)    Nature de l'engagement

Lorsque la somme versée pour la réservation est qualifiée d'acompte, l'engagement du bailleur et du locataire est DEFINITIF.

En conséquence, si l'une des parties refuse d'exécuter ses obligations, l'autre partie peut en demander l'exécution forcée de la réparation.

3.4   Annulation du contrat, le cas échéant

C'est seulement lorsque la somme versée pour la réservation constitue des arrhes que le locataire ou le bailleur peut se dédire aux conditions suivantes:

- le locataire en abandonnant au bailleur la somme versée;

- le bailleur en retournant au locataire le double de la somme reçue.

3.5   Loyer – Dépôt de garantie

Les montants du loyer, des taxes (droit de bail, taxe de séjour...) et charges éventuelles et du dépôt de garantie sont indiqués aux paragraphes 2.2, 2.3, 2.4, 2.5 et 2.6.

Dès son arrivée, à la remise des clés, le locataire versera entre les mains du bailleur une somme dont le montant est défini à 2.3, à titre de dépôt de garantie, pour répondre des dégâts qui pourraient être causés aux objets mobiliers ou autres garnissant les lieux loués.

Tout objet perdu, cassé, détérioré ou abîmé devra être remplacé ou remboursé au bailleur à sa valeur de remplacement par le locataire qui s'y oblige.

Ce dépôt de garantie, non productif d'intérêts, ne pourra en aucun cas être considéré comme le paiement d'une partie du loyer. Ce versement ne constitue pas des arrhes ni de dédit. En conséquence, les parties renoncent à se prévaloir des dispositions de l'article 1590 du Code Civil.

Il sera remboursé après restitution des clés et après déduction, s'il y a lieu, des réparations locatives, au départ du locataire ou au plus tard dans les 60 jours de son départ (arrêté du 8 janvier 1993).

Une somme forfaitaire sera éventuellement retenue pour le nettoyage des locaux; son montant est défini aux conditions particulières figurant à 2.6.

la restitution des clés au bailleur, en fin de location, n'emporte pas renonciation du bailleur à des indemnités pour réparations locatives, s'il prouve que les dommages sont le fait du locataire.

3.6    Couchage

Les locaux faisant l'objet de la présente location ne doivent, sous aucun prétexte, être occupés par un nombre de personnes supérieur à celui indiqué aux conditions particulières, sauf accord préalable et écrit du bailleur.

Le cas échéant, le bailleur pourra réclamer un supplément de loyer, ou refuser l'entrée dans les lieux.

3.7    Assurance

Le locataire doit être assuré à une compagnie d'assurances notoirement connue contre les risques de vol, incendie et dégât des eaux, tant pour ses risques locatifs que pour le mobilier donné en location, ainsi que pour les recours des voisins, et en justifier à première réquisition du bailleur.

En conséquence, ce dernier décline toute responsabilité pour le recours que sa compagnie d'assurance pourrait exercer contre le locataire en cas de sinistre.

3.8    Obligations principales du locataire

Il est tenu de

(a)    N'occuper les lieux que bourgeoisement, à l'exclusion de l'exercice de tout commerce, profession ou industrie, le locataire reconnaissant que cette location ne lui est consentie QU'A TITRE DE RESIDENCE PROVISOIRE ET DE PLAISANCE, condition majeure sans laquelle la présente location ne lui aurait pas été consentie.

(b)    Ne rien faire qui, de son fait ou du fait de sa famille ou de ses relations, puisse nuire à la tranquillité du voisinage ou des autres occupants.

(c)    En cas de location dans un immeuble collectif, se conformer en qualité d'occupant des lieux, au règlement intérieur de l'immeuble, dont il prendra connaissance par VOIE D'AFFICHAGE ou sur COMMUNICATION DU BAILLEUR.

(d)    Occuper les lieux personnellement et ne pouvoir EN AUCUN CAS sous-louer-même gratuitement, ni céder ses droits à la présente location, sauf accord écrit du bailleur.

(e)     Ne pouvoir sous aucun prétexte entreposer des meubles meublants, exception faite pour le linge et menus objets.

(f)     Ne faire aucune modification ni changement dans la disposition des meubles et des lieux.

(g)     N'introduire aucun animal familial (chiens, chats...) dans les locaux loués sans autorisation préalable et écrit du bailleur, la possibilité de détention étant subordonnée au fait que l'animal ne cause aucun dégât à l'immeuble, ni aucun trouble de jouissance dans le voisinage.

(h)     Laisser exécuter pendant la location, dans les lieux loués, les travaux dont l'urgence manifeste ne permet pas leur report.

(i)     Entretenir les lieux loués, et les rendre en bon état de propreté et de réparations locatives en fin de jouissance.

(j)     Informer immédiatement le bailleur de tout sinistre et des dégradations se produisant dans les lieux loués, même s'il n'en résulte aucun dommage apparent.

(k)     Répondre des dégradations et pertes qui arrivent par son propre fait ou par le fait des personnes de sa maison, pendant la jouissance du local, à moins qu'il ne prouve qu'elles ont eu lieu sans sa faute ni celle des personnes susdésignées.

(l)     Prévenir à l'avance du jour et de l'heure de son arrivée.

(m)     PRENDRE RENDEZ-VOUS POUR LES FORMALITES DE SORTIE TROIS JOURS AVANT SON DEPART.

3.9     Obligations principales du bailleur

Il est tenu de:

(a)     Délivrer les lieux loués en bon état d'usage et de réparations, ainsi que les équipements mentionnés au contrat en bon état de fonctionnement.

(b)     Assurer au locataire la jouissance paisible des lieux loués et le garantir des vices et défauts de nature à y faire obstacle.

(c)     Entretenir les locaux en état de servir à l'usage prévu.

(d)   Sauf urgence manifeste, ne pas effectuer de travaux dans les lieux loués pendant la durée de la location; tous travaux entraîneront dédommagement du locataire, pour les troubles de jouissance subis.

(e)   En cas de location dans un immeuble collectif, COMMUNIQUER au locataire le règlement intérieur de l'immeuble ou l'AFFICHER DANS LES PARTIES COMMUNES DE L'IMMEUBLE.

3.10  Election de domicile

Pour l'exécution des présentes, les parties font élection de domicile à l'immeuble en France.

4.  Informations pratiques

4.1   Comment réserver?

Le candidat locataire devra renvoyer le présent contrat dûment signé et accompagné de la somme demandée pour la réservation. **Attention!** S'il s'agit d'une location classée, cette somme constitue des arrhes; s'il s'agit d'une location non classée, cette somme est, au choix des parties, soit un acompte, soit des arrhes.

4.2   Organisation de l'arrivée

Le locataire devra prévenir à l'avance du jour, ainsi que de l'heure approximative de son arrivée, et faire en sorte de se présenter les jours ouvrables.

A la remise des clés, le solde de la location ainsi que le montant du dépôt de garantie prévus lui seront demandés.

4.3   Organisation du départ

Sauf accord préalable du bailleur, les locaux devront être libérés au plus tard pour le jour et l'heure prévus au 2.1.

4.4   Etat des lieux et inventaire du mobilier

L'état des lieux et l'inventaire détaillé du mobilier sont établis contradictoirement entre les parties à l'entrée dans les lieux du locataire et à la libération des locaux par le locataire, **sur rendez-vous préalable**.

Le cas échéant, le locataire a un délai de 3 jours pour contester l'état des lieux lors de son arrivée ou de son départ.

S'il n'a pas été fait l'état des lieux, le locataire est présumé avoir reçu les lieux loués en bon état de réparations locatives et doit les rendre tels sauf la preuve contraire (Article 1731 du Code Civil).

5. Signature des parties

Mots rayés:

Lignes rayées:

Fait et signé à ..................................... le ..................................... en .....................................
originaux dont un remis à chacune des parties qui le reconnaît.

Le bailleur ou son mandataire .........................................................................................
(signature précédée de la mention manuscrite 'lu et approuvé')

Le(s) Locataire(s) .........................................................................................
(signature précédée de la mention manuscrite 'lu et approuvé)

ATTENTION

Veuillez signer et dater séparement chaque exemplaire

## A.3 FRENCH FURNISHED LETTING AGREEMENT FOR A DURATION OF SIX MONTHS OR LONGER

Contrat de location meublée à usage d'habitation secondaire

Exclu du champ d'application de la loi n° 89-462 du 6 juillet 1989

Entre les soussignés: . . . . . . . . . . . . . . . . . . . . . . . . . . . . . . . . . . . . . . . . . . . . . . . . . . . . .

dénommé(s) 'Le Bailleur' en singulier

Mandataire (le cas échéant):

et . . . . . . . . . . . . . . . . . . . . . . . . . . . . . . . . . . . . . . . . . . . . . . . . . . . . . . . . . . . . . . . .

dénommé(s) 'Le Locataire' en singulier

Il a été convenu et arrêté ce qui suit:

Le Bailleur loue les locaux et équipements ci-après désignés au Locataire qui les accepte aux conditions suivantes:

1. Locaux

   Adresse:

   Consistance: Appartement/maison individuelle

   Dépendances:

   Garage n°

   Place de stationnement n°

   Cave n°

   Désignation des locaux et équipements privatifs:

   Enumération des parties et équipements communs:

   Gardiennage

   Interphone

   Ascenseur

   Vide-ordures

   Antenne T.V. collective

   Espace(s) vert(s)

   Chauffage collectif

   Eau chaude collective

2. Régime juridique

   En cas de contestation, compétence exclusive est attribuée aux Tribunaux Français.

   Le présent contrat de location est régi par les dispositions des articles 1714 à 1762 du Code Civil relatives aux baux d'immeubles à usage d'habitation ainsi que par les conditions prévues aux pages suivantes. Conclu dans le cadre de l'une des exclusions prévues à l'article 2 de la loi n° 89-462 du 6 juillet 1989, il n'est soumis ni aux dispositions de cette loi ni à celles prévues par la loi n° 48-1360 du 1 septembre 1948.

En conséquence, la durée du présent contrat de location ainsi que le montant du loyer sont librement fixés entre les parties.

Outre les conditions générales, le présent contrat de location est consenti et accepté aux prix, charges et conditions suivantes:

3.  Durée du contrat (cf Conditions Générales Chapitre I):

    Le présent contrat est conclu pour une durée de .............................. renouvelable ensuite par tacite reconduction et par périodes de faute de congé préalable.

4.  Date de prise d'effet

    Le contrat prendra effet le ...................................................

5.  Montant des paiements (cf Conditions Générales Chapitres III et IV)

    Loyer mensuel (somme en toutes lettres): ....................Frs

    Taxe (droit de bail): ....................Frs

    Charges mensuelles: ....................Frs

    Total mensuel: ....................Frs

6.  Termes de paiement

    Cette somme sera payable d'avance et en totalité le ........................... de chaque mois, entre les mains du Bailleur, soit de ...........................

7.  Révision du loyer (cf Conditions Générales Chapitre III)

    Le loyer sera révisé chaque année le ........................................

    Indice de référence: .......................................................

    Trimestre 200........

    Valeur:

8.  Dépôt de garantie (cf Conditions Générales Chapitre V)

    Cette somme (en toutes lettres) correspond à .................................. mois de loyer.

9.  Clause particulière (le cas échéant)

10. Honoraires (le cas échéant, cf Conditions Générales Chapitre XII)

Honoraires de négociations: . . . . . . . . . . . . . .Frs

Honoraires de rédaction: . . . . . . . . . . . . . .Frs

Frais d'état des lieux: . . . . . . . . . . . . . .Frs

Total: . . . . . . . . . . . . . .Frs

Conformément aux usages locaux, ces frais seront à la charge du Bailleur/Locataire.

11. Documents annexés

Etat des lieux établi lors de la remise des clés au Locataire (contradictoire ou par huissier).

Liste des réparations locatives fixées par le décret n° 87-712 du 26 août 1987.

Liste des charges récupérables fixées par le décret n° 87-713 du 26 août 1987.

Inventaire du mobilier

Acte de caution solidaire, le cas échéant.

12. Clés remises

Nombre de clés remises au locataire:

13. Signature des parties

Mots rayés:

Lignes rayées:

Fait et signé à ........... le ........... en ........... originaux dont un remis à chacune des parties qui le reconnaît.

Le Bailleur ou son Mandataire:

(Signature précédée de la mention manuscrite 'lu et approuvé')

Le Locataire:

(Signature précédée de la mention manuscrite 'lu et approuvé.')

La Caution

(Signature précédée de la mention manuscrite ' lu et approuvé. Je reconnais avoir reçu un exemplaire du présent contrat pour lequel je me pose caution par acte séparé et annexé.')

## CONDITIONS GÉNÉRALES

### I. *Durée (la date du contrat et sa date de prise d'effet sont indiquées en page 3)*

La durée du contrat, indiquée en page ..........., est librement fixée entre les parties.

Si le logement faisant l'objet de la présente location est loué ou attribué en raison de l'exercice d'une fonction ou de l'occupation d'un emploi, la durée du présent contrat sera indissociable de celle du contrat de travail. En conséquence, si le contrat de travail vient à être dénoncé ou rompu, la présente location sera automatiquement résiliée dans les mêmes conditions.

### II. *Résiliation*

Le contrat pourra être résilié par lettre recommandée avec avis de réception ou par acte d'huissier:

● Par le Locataire, à tout moment, en prévenant le bailleur trois mois à l'avance, délai ramené à un mois en cas de mutation, de perte d'emploi ou de nouvel emploi consécutif à une perte d'emploi.

● Par le Bailleur, en prévenant le Locataire trois mois avant le terme du contrat ou avant le terme de chacune des tacites reconductions.

### III. *Loyer*

Le montant du loyer, librement fixé entre les parties, sera payable au domicile du Bailleur ou de la personne qu'il aurait mandatée à cet effet. Il sera révisé chaque année en fonction de l'indice national I.N.S.E.E. du coût de la construction dont les éléments de référence sont indiqués en page 3.

### IV. *Charges*

En sus du loyer, le Locataire remboursera au Bailleur sa quote-part dans les charges réglementaires, conformément à la liste fixée par le décret n° 87-713 du 26 août 1987.

Les charges récupérables, sommes accessoires au loyer principal, sont exigibles en contrepartie:

● des services rendus liés à l'usage des différents éléments de la chose louée;

● des dépenses d'entretien courant et des menues réparations sur les éléments d'usage commun de la chose louée;

● du droit de bail et des impositions qui correspondent à des services dont le Locataire profite directement.

Elles seront réglées mensuellement, en même temps que le loyer principal.

**Contrat d'une durée supérieure à un an:**

Si le présent contrat est conclu pour une durée supérieure à un an, les charges mensuelles fixées en page 3 seront considérées comme des provisions devant faire l'objet d'une régularisation au moins annuelle.

Leur montant sera fixé chaque année par le Bailleur en fonction des dépenses réellement exposées l'année précédente ou du budget prévisionnel, le montant de chaque provision étant réajusté en conséquence.

Un mois avant l'échéance de la régularisation annuelle, le Bailleur adressera au Locataire un décompte par nature de charges ainsi que, dans les immeubles collectifs, le mode de répartition entre tous les locataires. Pendant ce mois, les pièces justificatives seront tenues à la disposition du Locataire.

**Contrat d'une durée maximale d'un an**

Par accord exprès entre les parties et dans un souci de simplification, si le présent contrat est conclu pour une durée maximale d'un an, les montants mensuels fixés en page 3 seront considérés comme des charges forfaitaires, apurant au fur et à mesure ce compte d'une façon définitive.

Cependant, si le contrat par le jeu de la tacite reconduction vient à dépasser la durée d'une année, dès ce seuil franchi, les charges devront être justifiées.

Les versements seront alors considérés comme des provisions devant faire l'objet de la régularisation annuelle selon les modalités prévues ci-avant pour les contrats d'une durée supérieure à un an.

*V.    Dépôt de garantie*

Le dépôt de garantie éventuellement versé par le Locataire afin de garantir la bonne exécution de ses obligations est équivalent à la période de loyer indiquée en page 4 et sera modifié de plein droit à chaque augmentation de loyer de manière à demeurer équivalent à cette période.

Ce dépôt, non productif d'intérêts, est indépendant des loyers et charges, lesquels devront être régulièrement payés aux dates fixées, jusqu'au départ effectif du Locataire. (Le départ étant entendu après complet déménagement, exécution des réparations locatives, résiliation des abonnements de gaz, électricité, eau et téléphone, présentation au Bailleur de la quittance taxe d'habitation, établissement de l'état des lieux contradictoire en fin de contrat et remise des clés).

Il sera restitué au Locataire en fin de jouissance, dans le mois suivant l'envoi par le syndic du relevé des comptes de charges de la période intéressée, déduction faite, le cas échéant, des sommes dûment justifiées restant dues au Bailleur ou dont celui-ci pourrait être tenu pour responsable aux lieux et place du Locataire.

## VI.    Etat des lieux (annexé au contrat)

Un état des lieux contradictoire sera établi lors de la remise des clés au Locataire et sera annexé aux présentes.

A défaut d'état des lieux, la présomption établie par l'article 1731 du Code Civil ne pourra être invoquée par celle des parties qui aura fait obstacle à l'établissement de l'état des lieux.

A la fin du contrat, lors de la restitution des clés par le Locataire, un état des lieux de sortie sera dressé contradictoirement entre les parties après rendez-vous pris avec le Bailleur huit jours à l'avance, à des heures ouvrables.

## VII.    Obligations du Bailleur

Le Bailleur est tenu des obligations principales suivantes:

1.    Délivrer au Locataire le logement en bon état d'usage et de réparations, ainsi que les équipements mentionnés au contrat en bon état de fonctionnement.

2.    Assurer au Locataire la jouissance paisible du logement et, sans préjudice des dispositions de l'article 1721 du Code Civil, le garantir des vices de construction ou du bon fonctionnement des équipements.

## VIII.    Obligations du Locataire

Le Locataire est tenu des obligations principales suivantes:

1.    Payer le loyer et les charges récupérables aux termes convenus. Le paiement mensuel est de droit s'il en fait la demande.

2.    User PAISIBLEMENT les locaux et équipements loués suivant la destination prévue au contrat.

3. Répondre des dégradations et pertes survenant pendant la durée du contrat dans les locaux dont il a la jouissance exclusive, à moins qu'il ne prouve qu'elles ont eu lieu par cas de force majeure, par la faute du Bailleur, ou par le fait d'un tiers qu'il n'a pas introduit dans le logement.

4. Prendre à sa charge l'entretien courant du logement et des équipements mentionnés au contrat, les menues réparations et l'ensemble des réparations locatives définies par le décret n° 87-712 du 26 août 1987, sauf si elles sont occasionnées par vétusté, malfaçon, vice de construction, cas forfait ou force majeure.

5. Souscrire un contrat d'entretien auprès d'une entreprise spécialisée (ou en rembourser le coût au Bailleur si ce dernier en assure le paiement) pour faire entretenir au moins une fois par an les équipements individuels (chauffage, gaz, brûleurs gaz...) et en justifier à première demande du Bailleur.

6. Informer immédiatement le Bailleur de tout sinistre et des dégradations se produisant dans les lieux loués, même s'il n'en résulte aucun dommage apparent.

7. Ne pas transformer sans l'accord écrit du Bailleur les locaux loués et leurs équipements: le Bailleur pourra, si le Locataire a méconnu cette obligation, exiger la remise en état des locaux et des équipements au départ du locataire ou conserver les transformations effectuées sans que le Locataire puisse réclamer une indemnité pour les frais engagés. Le Bailleur aura toutefois la faculté d'exiger aux frais du Locataire la remise immédiate des lieux en l'état si les transformations mettent en péril le bon fonctionnement des équipements ou la sécurité du local.

8. Laisser exécuter dans les lieux loués les travaux d'amélioration des parties communes ou des parties privatives du même immeuble, ainsi que les travaux nécessaires au maintien et état et à l'entretien normal des locaux loués: les dispositions des deuxième et troisième aliénas de l'article 1724 du Code Civil étant applicables à ces travaux.

9. Ne faire installer et ne faire usage d'aucun nouveau système de chauffage sans avoir vérifié à ses frais, et sous sa responsabilité, la conformité des cheminées avec les règles de sécurité en vigueur.

   Faire le ramonage des cheminées à ses frais, au moins une fois l'an et en fin de jouissance.

10. Respecter le règlement intérieur de l'immeuble affiché dans les parties communes des immeubles collectifs.

    Se conformer à toutes demandes ou instructions pouvant être formulées par le Bailleur en vertu des décisions d'assemblées générales des copropriétaires ou du règlement intérieur de l'immeuble et en exécuter strictement toutes les dispositions.

11. S'assurer contre les risques locatifs dont il doit répondre en sa qualité de Locataire: incendie, dégât des eaux etc, et en justifier au Bailleur à la remise des clés, en lui transmettant l'attestation émise par son assureur ou son représentant. Il devra en justifier ainsi chaque année, à la demande du Bailleur.

12. Occuper personnellement les lieux loués; ne pas céder le contrat de location, ni sous-louer le logement sauf avec accord écrit du Bailleur, y compris sur le prix du loyer. En cas de cessation du contrat principal, le sous-locataire ne pourra se prévaloir d'aucun droit à l'encontre du Bailleur, ni d'aucun titre d'occupation.

13. Laisser visiter, en vue de la vente ou de la location, les lieux loués deux heures par jour pendant les jours ouvrables. L'horaire de visite sera défini par accord entre les parties: à défaut d'accord, les visites auront lieu entre 17 h et 19 h.

14. Répondre de la perte ou de la détérioration des meubles mis à sa disposition par le Bailleur et dont l'inventaire est joint aux présentes; s'interdire absolument de transporter le mobilier hors des lieux loués.

15. Ne pas déménager, sans être conformé à ses obligations (paiement des loyers, des charges et des contributions diverses lui incombant personnellement, relevé des différents compteurs, exécution des réparations locatives etc), ni sans avoir auparavant présenté au Bailleur les quittances justifiant du paiement de la taxe d'habitation.

16. Remettre au Bailleur, dès son départ, toutes les clés des locaux loués et lui faire connaître sa nouvelle adresse.

## IX.     *Clause résolutoire et clauses pénales*

Le présent contrat sera RESILIE IMMEDIATEMENT ET DE PLEIN DROIT un mois après un commandement demeuré infructueux, sans qu'il soit besoin de faire ordonner cette résolution en justice, dans les cas suivants:

● à défaut de paiement aux termes convenus de tout ou partie du loyer et des charges;

● en cas de non versement du dépôt de garantie éventuellement prévu au contrat;

● en cas d'inexécution de l'une quelconque des conditions du présent contrat, qui sont toutes de rigueur;

- à défaut d'assurance contre les risques locatifs ou à défaut de justification au bailleur à chaque période convenue.

Une fois acquis au Bailleur le bénéfice de la clause résolutoire, le locataire devra libérer immédiatement les lieux; s'il refuse, son expulsion aura lieu sur simple ordonnance de référé.

Il est bien entendu qu'en cas de paiement par chèque, le loyer ne sera considéré comme réglé qu'après encaissement.

En outre, et sans qu'il soit dérogé à la précédente clause résolutoire, le Locataire s'engage formellement à respecter les deux clauses pénales qui suivent:

1. En cas de non paiement du loyer ou de ses accessoires aux termes convenus, et dès le premier acte d'huissier, le Locataire supportera une majoration de plein droit de 10% sur le montant des sommes dues, en dédommagement du préjudice subi par le Bailleur, et ce sans qu'une mise en demeure soit nécessaire, en dérogation à l'article 1230 du Code Civil.

2. Si le Locataire déchu de tout droit d'occupation ne libère pas les lieux, résiste à une ordonnance d'expulsion ou obtient des délais pour son départ, il devra verser par jour de retard, outre les charges, une indemnité conventionnelle d'occupation égale à deux fois le loyer quotidien, ceci jusqu'à complet déménagement et restitution des clés.

Cette indemnité est destinée à dédommager le Bailleur du préjudice provoqué par l'occupation abusive des lieux loués faisant obstacle à l'exercice des droits du Bailleur.

## X.  Tolérances

Il est formellement convenu que toutes les tolérances de la part du Bailleur, relatives aux conditions énoncées ci-dessus, qu'elles qu'en aient été la fréquence et la durée, ne pourront en aucun cas être considérées comme apportant une modification ou suppression de ces conditions, ni génératrices d'un droit quelconque. Le Bailleur pourra toujours y mettre fin à tout moment.

## XI.  Solidarité – Indivisibilité – Election de domicile

Pour l'exécution de toutes les obligations résultant du présent contrat, il y aura solidarité et indivisibilité entre:

- les parties ci-dessus désignées sous le vocable 'le Locataire';

- les héritiers ou représentants du Locataire venant à décéder (sous réserve de l'article 802 du Code Civil).

Cependant le contrat sera résilié immédiatement et de plein droit en cas de décès du Locataire bénéficiant du logement en raison de l'exercice d'une profession ou de l'exécution d'un contrat de travail.

Les parties signataires font élection de domicile; le Bailleur en sa demeure et le Locataire des lieux loués.

## XII.  *Frais – Honoraires*

Les honoraires éventuels de négociation et de rédaction des présentes ainsi que la ou les parties à qui en incombe la charge sont indiqués en page 4.

Les frais, droits et honoraires qui en seront la suite ou la conséquence, seront à la charge du Locataire qui s'y oblige. Il en sera de même pour les honoraires et frais consécutifs au recouvrement des loyers et charges par voie d'huissier ou de justice.

# ANNEXE A

## LISTE DE RÉPARATIONS LOCATIVES FIXÉES PAR LE DÉCRET N° 87-712 DU 26 AOÛT 1987

*1.*    *Parties extérieures dont le Locataire à l'usage exclusif*

a) **Jardins privatifs**

Entretien courant, notamment des allées, pelouses, massifs, bassins et piscines; taille, échenillage des arbres et arbustes. Remplacement des arbustes; réparation et remplacement des installations mobiles d'arrosage.

b) **Auvents, terrasses et marquises**

Enlèvement de la mousse et des autres végétaux.

c) **Descentes d'eau pluviale, chéneaux et gouttières**

Dégorgement des conduits.

*2.*    *Ouvertures intérieures et extérieures*

a) **Sections ouvrantes telles que portes et fenêtres**

Graissage des gonds, paumelles et charnières. Menues réparations des boutons et poignées de portes, des gonds, crémones et espagnolettes; remplacement notamment de boulons, clavettes et targettes.

b) **Vitrages**

Réfection des mastics. Remplacement des vitres détériorées.

c) **Dispositifs d'occulation de la lumière tels que stores et jalousies**

Graissage; remplacement notamment de cordes, poulies ou de quelques lames.

d) **Serrures et verrous de sécurité**

Graissage; remplacement de petites pièces ainsi que des clés égarées ou détériorées.

e) **Grilles**

Nettoyage et graissage; remplacement notamment de boulons, clavettes et targettes.

## 3. Parties intérieures

### a) Plafonds, murs intérieurs et cloisons

Maintien en état de propreté; menus raccords de peintures et tapisseries; remise en place ou remplacement de quelques éléments des matériaux de revêtement tels que faïence, mosaïque, matière plastique; rebouchage des trous rendu assimilable à une réparation par le nombre, la dimension et l'emplacement de ceux-ci.

### b) Parquets, moquettes et autres revêtements de sol

Encaustiquage et entretien courant de la vitrification; remplacement de quelques lames de parquets et remise en état, pose de raccords de moquettes et autres revêtements de sol, notamment en cas de taches et de trous.

### c) Placards et menuiseries telles que plinthes, baguettes et moulures

Remplacement des tablettes et tasseaux de placard et réparation de leur dispositif de fermeture; fixation de raccords et remplacement de pointes de menuiseries.

## 4. Installations de plomberie

### a) Canalisations d'eau

Dégorgement; remplacement notamment de joints et de colliers.

### b) Canalisations de gaz

Entretien courant de robinets, siphons et ouvertures d'aération; remplacement périodique des tuyaux souples de raccordement. Vidange.

### c) Chauffage, production d'eau chaude et robinetterie

Remplacement des bilames, pistons, membranes, boîtes à eau, allumage piézo-éléctrique, clapets et joints des appareils à gaz; rinçage et nettoyage des corps de chauffe et tuyauteries; remplacement des joints, clapets et presse-étoupes des robinets; remplacement des joints, flotteurs et joints closes des chasses d'eau.

### d) Eviers et appareils sanitaires

Nettoyage des dépôts de calcaire, remplacement des tuyaux flexibles de douches.

**5.** ***Equipement d'installations d'électricité***

Remplacement des interrupteurs, prises de courant, coupe-circuits et fusibles, des ampoules, tubes lumineux; réparation ou remplacement des baguettes ou gaines de protection.

**6.** ***Autres équipements mentionnés au contrat de location***

a)  Entretien courant et menues réparations des appareils tels que réfrigérateurs, machines à laver de linge et de vaisselle, sèche-linge, hottes aspirantes, adoucisseurs, capteurs solaires, pompes à chaleur, appareils de conditionnement d'air, antennes individuelles de radiodiffusion et de télé-vision, meubles scellés, cheminées, glaces et miroirs.

b)  Menues réparations nécessitées par la dépose des bourrelets.

c)  Graissage et remplacement des joints des vidoirs.

d)  Ramonage des conduits d'évacuation des fumées et des gaz et conduits de ventilation.

## ANNEXE B

## LISTE DE CHARGES RÉCUPÉRABLES FIXÉES PAR LE DÉCRET N° 87-713 DU 26 AOÛT 1987

1. **ASCENSEURS ET MONTE-CHARGE**

**1.1** *Dépenses d'électricité*

**1.2** *Dépenses d'exploitation, d'entretien courant, de menues réparations:*

a) Exploitation

- visite périodique, nettoyage et graissage des organes mécaniques;

- examen semestriel des câbles et vérification annuelle des parachutes;

- nettoyage annuel de la cuvette, du dessus de la cabine et de la machinerie;

- dépannage ne nécessitant pas de réparations ou fournitures de pièces;

- tenue d'un dossier par l'entreprise d'entretien mentionnant les visites techniques, incidents et faits importants touchant l'appareil.

b) Fournitures relatives à des produits ou à du petit matériel d'entretien (chiffons, graisses et huiles nécessaires) et aux lampes d'éclairage de la cabine.

c) Menues réparations

- de la cabine (boutons d'envoi, paumelles de portes, contacts de portes, fermes-portes automatiques, coulisseaux de cabine, dispositif de sécurité de treuil et cellule photo-électriques);

- des paliers (ferme-portes mécaniques, électriques ou pneumatiques, serrures électromécaniques, contacts de porte et boutons d'appel);

- des balais du moteur et fusibles.

2. **EAU FROIDE, EAU CHAUDE ET CHAUFFAGE COLLECTIF DES LOCAUX PRIVATIFS ET DES PARTIES COMMUNES**

**2.1** *Dépenses relatives*

A l'eau froide et chaude des locataires ou occupants du bâtiment ou de l'ensemble des bâtiments d'habitation concernés;

A l'eau nécessaire à l'entretien courant des parties communes du ou desdits bâtiments, y compris la station d'épuration;

A l'eau nécessaire à l'entretien courant des espaces extérieurs;

Les dépenses relatives à la consommation d'eau incluent l'ensemble des taxes et redevances ainsi que les sommes dues au titre de la redevance d'assainissement, à l'exclusion de celles auxquelles le propriétaire est astreint en application de l'article L.35-5 du Code de la Santé publique;

Aux produits nécessaires à l'exploitation, à l'entretien et au traitement de l'eau;

A l'électricité;

Au combustible ou à la fourniture, quelle que soit sa nature.

### 2.2 *Dépenses d'exploitation, d'entretien courant et de menues réparations*

a) **Exploitation et entretien courant:**

- nettoyage des gicleurs, électrodes, filtres et clapets des brûleurs;

- entretien courant et graissant des pompes de relais, jauges, contrôleurs de niveau ainsi que des groupes motopompes et pompes de puisards;

- graissage des vannes et robinets et réfection des presse- étoupes;

- remplacement des ampoules, des voyants lumineux et ampoules de chaufferie;

- entretien et réglage des appareils de régulation automatique et de leurs annexes;

- vérification et entretien des régulateurs de tirage;

- réglage des vannes, robinets et tés ne comprenant pas l'équilibrage;

- purge des points de chauffage;

- frais de contrôle de combustion;

- entretien des épurateurs de fumée;

- opérations de mise en repos en fin de saison de chauffage, rinçage des corps de chauffe et tuyauteries, nettoyage de chaufferies, y compris leurs puisards et siphons, ramonage des chaudières, carneaux et cheminées;

- conduite de chauffage;

- frais de location, d'entretien et de relevé des compteurs généraux et individuels;

- entretien de l'adoucisseur, du détartreur d'eau, du surpresseur et du détendeur;

- contrôles périodiques visant à éviter les fuites de fluide frigorigène des pompes de chaleur;

- vérification, nettoyage et graissage des organes des pompes à chaleur;

- nettoyage périodique de la face extérieure des capteurs solaires;

- vérification, nettoyage et graissage des organes des capteurs solaires.

b) **Menues réparations dans les parties communes ou sur des éléments d'usage commun:**

- réparation des fuites sur raccords et joints;

- remplacement des joints, clapets et presse-étoupes;

- rodage des sièges de clapets;

- menues réparations visant à remédier aux fuites de fluide frigorigène des pompes à chaleur;

- recharge en fluide frigorigène des pompes à chaleur.

## 3. INSTALLATIONS INDIVIDUELLES

Chauffage et production d'eau chaude, distribution d'eau dans les parties privatives:

### 3.1 *Dépenses d'alimentation commune de combustible*

### 3.2 *Exploitation et entretien courant, menues réparations*

a) Exploitation et entretien courant

- réglage de débit et température de l'eau chaude sanitaire;

- vérification et réglage des appareils de commande, d'asservissement, de sécurité d'aquastat et de pompe;

- dépannage;

- contrôle des raccordements et de l'alimentation des chauffe-eau électriques, contrôle de l'intensité absorbée;

- vérification de l'état des résistances, des thermostats, nettoyage;

- réglage des thermostats et contrôle de la température d'eau;

- contrôle et réfection d'étanchéité des raccordements eau froide eau chaude;

- contrôle des groupes de sécurité;

- rodage des sièges de clapets des robinets;

- réglage des mécanismes de chasses d'eau.

b) **Menues réparations**

- remplacement des bilames, pistons, membranes, boîtes à eau, allumage piézo-électrique, clapets et joints des appareils à gaz;

- rinçage et nettoyage des corps de chauffe et tuyauteries;

- remplacement des joints, clapets et presse-étoupes des robinets;

- remplacement des joints, flotteurs et joints cloches des chasses d'eau.

## 4. PARTIES COMMUNES INTÉRIEURES AU BÂTIMENT OU À L'ENSEMBLE DES BÂTIMENTS D'HABITATION

### 4.1 *Dépenses relatives*

- à l'électricité;

- aux fournitures consommables, notamment produits d'entretien, balais et petit matériel assimilé nécessaires à l'entretien de propreté, sel.

### 4.2 *Exploitation et entretien courant, menues réparations*

- entretien de la minuterie, pose, dépose et entretien des tapis;

- menues réparations des appareils d'entretien de propreté tels qu'aspirateur.

### 4.3 *Entretien de propreté (frais de personnel)*

## 5. ESPACES EXTÉRIEURS AU BÂTIMENT OU À L'ENSEMBLE DES BÂTIMENTS D'HABITATION (VOIES DE CIRCULATION, AIRES DE STATIONNEMENT, ABORDS ET ESPACES VERTS, AIRES ET ÉQUIPEMENTS DE JEUX).

### 5.1 Dépenses relatives

- à l'électricité;

- à l'essence et l'huile;

- aux fournitures consommables utilisées dans l'entretien courant: ampoules ou tubes d'éclairage, engrais, produits bactéricides et insecticides, produits tels que graines, fleurs, plants, plantes de remplacement, à l'exclusion de celles utilisées pour la réfection de massifs, plates-bandes ou haies.

### 5.2 Exploitation et entretien courant

Opérations de coupe, désherbage, sarclage, ratissage, nettoyage et arrosage concernant:

- les allées aires de stationnement et abords;

- les espaces verts (pelouses, massifs, arbustes, haies vives, plates-bandes);

- les aires de jeux;

- les bassins, fontaines, caniveaux, canalisations d'évacuation des eaux pluviales;

- entretien du matériel horticole;

- remplacement du sable des bacs et du petit matériel de jeux;

- peinture et menues réparations des bancs de jardin et des équipements de jeux et grillages.

## 6. HYGIÈNE

### 6.1 Dépenses de fournitures consommables

- sacs en plastique et en papier nécessaires à l'élimination des rejets;

- produits relatifs à la désinsectisation et à la désinfection, y compris des colonnes sèches de vide-ordures.

*6.2*    *Exploitation et entretien courant*

● entretien et vidange des fosses d'aisances;

● entretien des appareils de conditionnement des ordures.

*6.3*    *Elimination des rejets (frais de personnel)*

**7.**    **EQUIPEMENT DIVERS DU BÂTIMENT OU DE L'ENSEMBLE DES BÂTIMENTS D'HABITATION**

*7.1*    *La fourniture nécessaire à la ventilation mécanique*

*7.2*    *Exploitation et entretien courant*

● ramonage des conduits de ventilation;

● entretien de la ventilation mécanique;

● entretien des dispositifs d'ouverture automatique ou codée et des interphones;

● visites périodiques à l'exception des contrôles réglementaires de sécurité, nettoyage et graissage de l'appareillage fixe de manutention des nacelles de nettoyage des façades vitrées.

*7.3*    *Divers*

● abonnement des postes de téléphone à la disposition des locataires.

**8.**    **IMPOSITIONS ET REDEVANCES**

● droit de bail;

● taxe ou redevance d'enlèvement des ordures ménagères;

● taxe de balayage.

# APPENDIX B: TYPICAL INCOME TAX COMPUTATION

## PROPERTY RENTAL BY NON-RESIDENT

1. Mr and Mrs Frank O'File are non-French resident individuals who own a home in the Dordogne. The value of the property (buildings only) is FrF 800,000. The property is in fact let out on a furnished basis from time to time and produced a rental income of FrF 120,000 in 2000. The couple occupied the property for 1 month, for which the rental value is estimated at FrF 4,800. They paid FrF 6,000 in *taxes foncières,* FrF 4,000 in *taxe d'habitation* and FrF 25,000 for repairs and maintenance during the year. They have no other French sources of income, but substantial income from sources outside France. They are married with two minor children. Their country of residence has concluded a full double tax treaty with France (*Note 1*).

2. Because they are letting the property on a furnished basis, Mr & Mrs O'File's French source income will be assessed under business income rules and not as rental income. But since their rental income does not exceed FrF 500,000, they will be assessed under the *Micro BIC* regime for calculation of their taxable income.

3. They will not be considered to be 'professional landlords' because their rental income is less than FrF 150,000 per annum and it does not constitute the greater part of their income. Apart from certain consequences in terms of the availability of relief for any losses on the lettings, which are unlikely to concern Mr and Mrs O'File, the main consequence of not being 'professional landlords' is that any gain on an eventual disposal of the property will be taxed as a private capital gain and not as a business gain.

4. Theoretically, if they elected to have their business income calculated under the rules for the 'real' regime, the O'Files would still be able to claim depreciation on the buildings as a business expense, provided that the property was included in the balance sheet of the business. However if it were so included, they would have to declare a rent for the period that they occupied the property. On the assumptions that they choose to be assessed under the *Micro BIC* rules, their income tax liability for 2000, payable in 2001, will be computed as follows:

| Income of 2000 | FrF | FrF |
|---|---|---|
| Rental income (*Note 2*) | | 120,000 |
| Less:  Global deduction for expenses (70%) | | 84,000 |
| | | FrF 36,000 |
| Minimum income tax liability for non-residents at 25% (*Note 1*) | | FrF 9,000 |

*Note 1.  Because Mr & Mrs Frank O'File are resident in a country which has concluded a full double tax treaty with France, they are not subject to tax on a notional income of three times the annual rental value of the property. Correspondingly, however, their liability is subject to the minimum tax rate of 25%. If their liability calculated at scale rates exceeded the minimum liability, the normal scale rates would apply, but this will clearly not be the case in this example.*

*Note 2.  Mr & Mrs Frank O'File are not liable to pay any social contributions because they are not resident in France.*

*Note 3.  It does not matter whether the rent is paid to the couple by non-French residents or into a bank account outside France. The income is still French source income, and subject to tax in France.*

5.  *Mr & Mrs Frank O'File* would also pay the tax on leases (see 7.3.3).

6.  Generally a business of furnished lettings is not subject to the business tax (*taxe professionnelle*), unless the local government authorities have resolved that such businesses should pay this tax. There are areas of France where the *taxe professionnelle* is levied on landlords of furnished lettings.

# APPENDIX C:

# FRENCH-ENGLISH GLOSSARY FOR HOME BUYERS AND HOME OWNERS

| | |
|---|---|
| abandonner | to quit/surrender |
| abat-jour | lampshade |
| abattant | desk/table flap/leaf |
| abattement | allowance/rebate |
| abîmer | to damage/to spoil |
| abolir | to cancel |
| abonnement | standing charge/ subscription |
| abonner | to subscribe |
| abordable | affordable |
| aborder | to approach |
| abords | surroundings |
| abri | shed/shelter |
| abrogation | abolition/annulment/ cancellation |
| abus | abuse/breach |
| abus de droit | misuse of law |
| abusif | abusive |
| acajou | mahogany |
| accéder | to comply with |
| acceptation | acceptance |
| accès | access |
| accès pour handicapés | entrance for disabled |
| accessoires | ancillary/incidental |
| accolée | semi-detached |
| accord | agreement |
| accorder | to allow |
| accrochage | fixing/hanging up |
| accueil | reception/welcome |
| accumulateur | storage heater |
| acheminer | to channel |
| acheter | to buy |
| achèvement | completion |
| acier | steel |
| acier inoxydable | stainless steel |
| acompte | account/deposit/ instalment/ down payment |
| acoustique | acoustic |
| acquéreur | purchaser |
| acquiescement | acceptance |

| | |
|---|---|
| acquis | acquired/vested |
| acquittement | acquittal/discharge |
| acte de vente | deed of sale |
| acte notarié | notarised deed |
| acte sous seing privé | private written agreement |
| adaptation | adjustment |
| à debattre | negotiable |
| adoucisseur d'eau | water softener |
| aération | airing/ventilation |
| affaire | business/bargain |
| affaissement | subsidence |
| afférent | relating to |
| affermer | to lease |
| afficher | to advertise/post bills |
| agent immobilier | estate agent |
| agent locataire | letting agent |
| agglomération | built-up area |
| aggloméré | chipboard |
| agrandissement | extension |
| aléatoire | contingent |
| alimentaire | maintenance |
| allant au four | oven proof |
| allée | path |
| amélioration | improvement |
| aménagé | converted |
| ameublement | furniture |
| amovible | detachable/removable |
| ampèrage | current |
| ampoule (électrique) | light bulb |
| annexe | extension |
| annuler | to cancel |
| antenne | aerial |
| antidérapant | non-skid |
| appareil électroménager | domestic appliance |
| appartement | apartment/flat |
| appartenir | to belong to |
| appentis | lean-to |
| applique | wall lamp |

| | | | |
|---|---|---|---|
| apprêter | to prime | augmenter | to increase |
| appui de fenêtre | windowsill (inside) | autocuiseur | pressure cooker |
| arbre | tree | autorisation | planning permission |
| arbuste | bush/shrub | (de construire) | |
| architecte | landscape architect | auvent | awning/canopy |
| paysagiste | | avant-toit | eaves |
| architrave | architrave | avarie | damage |
| ardoise | slate | avenant | endorsement |
| are | 100 square metres | avertissement | caveat/notice/warning |
| armature à toit | roof truss | aveu | acknowledgement/ |
| armoire | wardrobe | | admission |
| arpenteur | surveyor | avis d'échéance | renewal notice |
| arrêt de façade | shutter fastening | | |
| arrhes | deposit | bac de douche | shower tray |
| arrière-cuisine | scullery | bâche | tarpaulin |
| arrière-pays | back country | badigeon | distemper |
| arrondissement | borough/district | baguette | trim/beading/ |
| arrosage | watering | | cable cover |
| arroseur | sprinkler | baignoire | bath |
| artisan | workman/craftsman | bail | lease/tenancy |
| artisanat | handicraft | | agreement |
| artisan carreleur | ceramic tiler | bailleur | landlord |
| artisan maçon | builder | balcon | balcony |
| asbeste | asbestos | banc | bench |
| ascendant | parent, grandparent etc | bardeau | shingle |
| ascenseur | lift | barrière | gate/barrier |
| aspect mat | matt finish | barrière | damp-proof course |
| aspect velouté | silk finish | anti-humidité | |
| aspect satiné | gloss finish | des remontées | |
| asphalte | asphalt | capillaires | |
| aspirateur | vacuum cleaner | bâtiment | building |
| assainissement | decontamination/ | bâtir | to build |
| | draining/purification | bêche | spade |
| assemblages | joints | bédane | mortise chisel |
| assignation | citation/notice/service | benne | skip |
| assise | base | béton | concrete |
| assujetti | liable/taxpayer | béton armé | reinforced concrete |
| assurance | insurance | bétonnière | cement mixer |
| assurance de | personal insurance | bibliothèque | bookcase |
| personnes | | bihebdomaire | bi-weekly |
| assurances | property insurance | bimensuel | bi-weekly |
| dommages | | biseau | bevel |
| atelier | shop/workshop | bitume | bitumen |
| atermoiemont | delay | blocaille | hardcore |
| âtre | hearth/fireplace | bloc-évier | sink unit |
| attestation | certificate | bois | wood |
| auge | mixing trough | bois blanc | deal |

| | | | |
|---|---|---|---|
| bois de construction | timber | câble de distribution | mains cable |
| bois dur | hardwood | cadastre | town planning registry |
| boiserie | woodwork | cadenas | padlock |
| bois massif | solid wood | cadre | frame |
| boisseau | chimney flue tile | caduc | null |
| bois tendre | soft wood | cailloux | pebbles |
| boîte | box/garage | calfeutrage | draft proofing |
| boîte à ordures | rubbish bin | cambriolage | burglary |
| boîte aux lettres | letter/post box | camion | lorry |
| boîte de dérivation | junction box | canalisation | pipeline |
| bord de mer | seaside | canapé | sofa |
| bord de rivière | riverside | canapé-lit | sofa-bed |
| borne | terminal | caniveau | gutter |
| bouche d'aération | air vent | caractéristique | feature |
| | | carelette | tile cutter |
| bouleau | birch | carie | rot |
| boulon | bolt | carie sèche | dry rot |
| bourrelet | beading/ draught excluder | carillon | doorbell |
| | | carreau de faïence | ceramic tile |
| bouton de porte | door knob | carreau de liège | cork tile |
| bricoleur | handyman | carreau de plâtre | plaster board |
| brique | brick/building block | carrelet | square ruler |
| brique à air | air brick | carrelage | tiling |
| brique creuse | hollow brick | carrière | quarry |
| brique réfractaire | fire-proof brick | carte de commerçant | traders card |
| briquetage | brickwork | | |
| brosse à maroufler | wallpaper brush | carte professionnelle | professional licence |
| brosse d'encollage | pasting brush | carton-cuir | hardboard |
| | | cautionnement | guarantee |
| brosse métallique | wire brush | cave | cellar |
| | | céder | to assign |
| brouette | wheelbarrow | cèdre | cedar |
| brouillon | draft | centre des impèts | tax office |
| broyeur à ordures | waste-disposal unit | | |
| buanderie | utility room | certificat de conformité | building regulation approval |
| buffet | sideboard | certificat d'urbanisme | outline planning permission |
| buffet de cuisine | kitchen cabinet | | |
| bureau des hypothêques | French land registry | cession | sale |
| butagaz | calor gas | cession de bail | ssignment of a lease |
| | | CGI | French tax law |
| cabinet | cabinet/office/ small room | (Code Général des Impôts) | |
| câble | cable | chalumeau | blow-lamp |

| | | | |
|---|---|---|---|
| chambranle | frame | ciseau de maçon | masonry chisel |
| chambre | room | citerne | water tank |
| chambre à coucher | bedroom | clapet | valve |
| Chambre de Commerce et d'Industrie | Chamber of Commerce | clef (à écrous) | spanner |
| | | clés | keys |
| | | clé à molette | adjustable spanner |
| Chambre des Métiers | Chamber of Trades | climatisation | air conditioning |
| | | cloison | partition/dividing wall |
| chambre d'hôte | guest house | cloison contre l'humidité | damp proof course |
| chambre mansardée | loft conversion | clôture | fence/enclosure |
| champ | field | clou | nail |
| chantier de construction | building site | clou à béton | masonry nail |
| | | clou cavalier | staple |
| chape | screed | clou de tapissier | carpet tack |
| charnière | hinge | Code Civil | French Civil Code |
| charpente | framework | Code de travail | French employment code |
| charpentier | carpenter | | |
| chasse d'eau | flush toilet | coin | corner/wedge |
| châtaigne | chestnut | coin du feu | ingle-nook |
| chaudière | boiler | coin-cuisine | kitchenette |
| chaudière à gaz | gas fired boiler | colle | glue |
| chaudière à mazout | oil fired boiler | colocataires | co-tenants |
| | | colombage | timber framed |
| chaudière à charbon | charcoal burning boiler | colonne | column |
| | | comble | loft |
| chauffage | heating | commerçant | commercial trader |
| chauffage au mazout | oil fired heating | commode | chest of drawers |
| | | commodités | lavatory |
| chauffage central | central heating | commun | common |
| | | complémentaire | further/supplementary |
| chauffage sous-sol | under-floor heating | comporter | to include |
| | | compromis de vente | contract |
| chauffe-eau | water heater | | |
| chaume | thatch | comptable | accountant |
| chaumière | thatched cottage | comptabilité | book keeping |
| chemin | path | compte rendu | report |
| cheminée | chimney/fireplace | compte séquestre | stakeholder account |
| chêne | oak | | |
| chéneau | gutter | compteur | meter |
| cheville | rawlplug | conception | design |
| chevron | rafter | concepteur | designer |
| ciment | cement | concierge | caretaker |
| ciseau à bois | wood chisel | condition suspensivea | condition precedent in contract |
| ciseau de briqueteur | brick/cold chisel | | |
| | | conduit | duct/shaft |

| | | | |
|---|---|---|---|
| conduit de cheminée | flue | coupe-circuit principal | main fuse |
| conduit de gaz | gas pipe | courant alternatif et continu | AC/DC |
| conduit d'évacuation | sewer | couteau universel | Stanley knife |
| conduite principale | water main | couvreur | roofer |
| | | crampon | staple |
| congé | notice | crémone | rotating handle on |
| congédier | to dismiss | | shutters and windows |
| congélateur | freezer | crèpe | stucco |
| conifère | conifer | crépi | rendering |
| conjoncteur | mains switch | crochet | door catch |
| conservatoire | conservatory | cuisine équipée | fitted kitchen |
| conserver | to retain | cuisinière | cooker |
| consignes en cas d'incendie | fire regulations | cuisinière à gaz | gas cooker |
| | | cumulus électrique | immersion heater |
| constat | declaration of damage | | |
| constat amiable | agreed accident report | cuvette | basin |
| constructeur | builder | cuvette de W C | toilet pan |
| construire | to build | | |
| contemporain | contemporary | dallage | paving |
| contestation | dispute | dalle | flag/paving stone/ quarry tile |
| contourner | to by-pass/circumvent | | |
| contrat | contract | dalles de miroir | mirror tiles |
| contrat d'assurances | insurance policy | débarras | box room |
| | | débouchage des canalisations | unblocking the drains |
| contrat de travail | employment contract | | |
| contravention | breach | décapant | paint stripper/scourer |
| contrecoeur | back-plate (of hearth) | déclaration annuelle | annual tax return |
| contremaître | foreman | | |
| contre-plaqué | plywood | décolleuse | paper stripper |
| convecteur | convector heater | décompte | account/breakdown/ statement |
| convention d'occupation précaire | licence | | |
| | | dédommagement | compensation |
| | | défaut d'entretien | maintenance failure |
| conversion | conversion | défaut de paiement | non payment |
| coordonnées téléphoniques | telephone number | | |
| | | défectueux | defective |
| corbeau | corbel | défonceuse | router |
| corniche | coving | défraîchi | faded |
| couche isolante | damp-proof course | dégager | to unblock |
| coude | plumbing bend | dégât | damage |
| coulage | substantial leak | dégorgement | discharge/overflow |
| coupe carreau | tile cutter | dégradations | degradation/erosion |
| coupe-circuit | fuse box | déhumidificateur | de-humidifier |
| coupe-circuit à fusible | fuse | déjeter | to warp |
| | | délai | time limit |

| | | | |
|---|---|---|---|
| délayage | padding | double vitrage | double glazing |
| démarches | formalities | douche | shower |
| déménagement | removal | douchette | shower rose |
| demeure | residence | douille | lampholder/light switch |
| dépannage | fixing/repairing | draps | sheet |
| dépareillé | incomplete/spoilt | draps de bain | large towels |
| dépendance | outbuilding | dresser | to prepare |
| dépenses | maintenance expenses | droit | law/right/tax |
| d'entretien | | droit de bail | tax on leases |
| dépôt de garantie | deposit | droit de passage | right of way |
| dépourvu | out of stock | droit de | pre-emption right |
| dérangement | inconvenience | préemption | |
| désaccord | dispute | droits de | French gifts tax |
| désagréments | disagreements | donation | |
| descriptif | descriptive/ | droits de | French inheritance tax |
| | explanatory letter | succession | |
| dessécher | to dry out | duplex | duplex apartment/ |
| désherbage | weeding | | maisonette |
| désignation | description | durée | length/period |
| desservi | served/supplied | | |
| dessin | drawing | eau | water |
| dessinateur | draftsman | eau de la ville | mains water |
| destination | permitted user | eau dure | hard water |
| des lieux | | eau pluviale | rainwater |
| détartrer | to descale | eaux d'égout | sewage |
| détecteur | detector | ébauche | rough sketch |
| détendeur | gas pressure regulator | ébéniste | cabinet maker |
| déversoir | overflow | ébruiter | to leak out |
| devis | estimate | échafaud | scaffold |
| devis descriptif | bill of quantities | échantillon | cross section/sample |
| diamant | glass cutter | échéance | deadline/expiration |
| disjoncteur | trip switch/circuit | échelle | ladder/scale |
| | breaker | échelle d'incendie | fire escape |
| dispense | waiver | échelle double | step ladder |
| disponible | available | éclairage | lighting |
| dissimulation | concealment/evasion/ | éclairage au | strip lighting |
| | witholding | néon | |
| divers | miscellaneous/sundry | écoulement | leak |
| dol | fraud | écrou | screw nut |
| doléance | grievance | écurie | stables |
| domaine | estate | EDF | French electricity |
| dommage | damage | | company |
| dommages- | damages and interest | égout | sewer |
| intérêts | | égout des toits | eaves |
| domicile | abode/home/residence | électrode | welding rod |
| domicile fiscal | tax residence | éléments | sanitary ware |
| double fenêtre | double glazing | sanitaire | |

| | | | |
|---|---|---|---|
| embaucher | to hire/employ | étayer | to shore up |
| empêchement | bar/disability/ obstruction | évacuation | waste water |
| | | évier | sink |
| empiéter | to trespass | expert immobilier | surveyor |
| emplacement | location/site | expertise | survey |
| encadrement | framing | expiration du bail | termination of a lease |
| encaisser | to bank | extincteur | fire extinguisher |
| encastré | built-in | extracteur | extractor |
| enclos | paddock | | |
| endommager | to damage | faire sauter les plombs | blow the fuses |
| enduit | plaster coating/ rendering/filler | | |
| | | fait des tiers | act of third parties |
| enfouchement | dovetailing | faïence | earthenwear |
| enlèvement | removal | faîte | ridge |
| enregistrement | registration of title | faîtière | ridge tile |
| en tontine | joint tenancy | fauteuil | armchair |
| entrebailleur à chaîne | security chain | faux plafond | false ceiling |
| | | femme de ménage | cleaning lady |
| entremise | maintenance | fenêtre | window |
| entretenir | to maintain/upkeep/ service | fenêtre à battants | casement window |
| | | fenêtre à guillotine | sash window |
| entretien | maintenance/upkeep | | |
| enveloppe | cylinder jacket | fenêtre treillagée | lattice window |
| envelopper | to lag/wrap | fer à souder | soldering iron |
| épaisseur | thickness | fer forgé | wrought iron |
| épave | wreck | ferme | farm/fixed |
| épurateur | purifier | fermette | small farm |
| équerre à dessin | set square | fermeture | catch/clasp/fastener |
| équerre droite | right angle | ferraillage | ironwork |
| équipements communs | shared facilities | ferronnerie | ironwork |
| | | feutre à toit | roofing felt |
| érable | maple | fibres dures | hardboard |
| escabeau | step ladder | fibrociment | synthetic roof tiles |
| escalier | staircase | fil | cable |
| escalier de secours | fire escape | fil à plomb | plumb-line |
| | | fil fusible | fuse wire |
| espagnolette | shutter/ window fastener | filtre | filter |
| | | finitions | finishing |
| établi | work bench | fisc | tax authorities |
| étage | storey | fixer un prix | to quote |
| étagère | shelves | fléchir | to sag |
| étanche | watertight | flotteur | ball cock |
| étang | lake/pond | foncier | to do with land/ property |
| état des lieux | schedule of condition | | |
| état des lieux de sortie | schedule of dilapidation | fonctionnement | operation/running |
| | | fondation | foundation |
| état moyen | average condition | | |

| French | English |
|--------|---------|
| fonds de commerce | business assets |
| fonds de clientèle | goodwill |
| fongible | soft |
| fongicide | fungicide |
| fonte | cast iron |
| force majeure | act of God |
| foret | drill |
| forêt | forest |
| foret pour le métal | metal drill |
| forfaitaire | fixed (amount) |
| forte agrafeuse | staple gun |
| fossé | ditch/gulf/cap |
| fosse d'aisance | cesspool |
| fosse septique | septic tank |
| four | oven |
| four à micro-ondes | microwave oven |
| fourneau à gaz | gas heater |
| fournisseur | supplier |
| foyer | hearth/fireplace |
| fraise | countersink |
| frêne | ash (wood) |
| frigidaire | fridge |
| front de mer | seashore |
| fuite | leak |
| fusible | fuse |
| fusible à cartouche | cartridge fuse |
| frigo | fridge |
| | |
| gâche | catch of a lock |
| gaine | sheathing |
| galvaniser | to galvanise |
| garde-corps | railings |
| garde-feu | fire guard |
| garde-robe | wardrobe |
| gardien | caretaker |
| garniture | upholstery |
| gaz | gas |
| gaz de ville | mains gas |
| gazon | turf/lawn |
| GDF | French gas company |
| gel | frost |
| géomètre expert | land surveyor |
| gérant | manager |
| gercement | chapping/cracking |
| gestation | management |
| glace | ice |
| gond | shutter hinge pin |
| goudron | tar |
| goulet d'étranglement | bottleneck |
| gouttière | gutter |
| graissage | greasing/lubricating |
| grandeur | size |
| grange | barn |
| graphique | chart/diagram/graph |
| grattoir | scraper |
| gravier | gravel |
| gravillons | loose chippings |
| grêle | hail |
| grenier | attic/loft/barn |
| grès | sandstone |
| griffe | tile scorer |
| gril | grill |
| grillage | wire netting/mesh |
| grille | gate/window grill |
| | |
| habileté | craft/expertise |
| habitation | dwelling |
| hache | axe |
| haie | hedge |
| hameau | hamlet |
| hangar | Dutch/open barn |
| hauteur libre | headroom |
| hebdomodaire | weekly |
| hébergement | accommodation/lodging |
| hectare | 2.2 acres |
| héritier | heir/beneficiary |
| hêtre | beech |
| heures creuses | off-peak |
| honoraires | fees |
| horloge | clock (large) |
| HT (hors taxe) | exclusive of tax |
| hors-cote | kerbstone |
| hors saison | out of season |
| housse | cover |
| huile | oil |
| huile de lin | linseed oil |
| humidificateur | humidifier |
| humidité | damp |

| | |
|---|---|
| huissier de justice | bailiff/process server |
| hypothèque | mortgage |
| | |
| if | yew |
| immatriculation | registration |
| immeubles | buildings |
| imperméable | waterproof |
| imposable | taxable |
| imposte | fanlight |
| impôt | tax |
| impôt de solidarité sur la fortune (ISF) | wealth tax |
| impôt sur les plus values | capital gains tax |
| impôt sur le revenu des personnes physiques (IRPP) | income tax |
| impôt sur les sociétés (IS) | corporation tax |
| imputation | charge/imputation |
| imprévu | contingency |
| improvisé | makeshift |
| incendie | arson/fire |
| indemnité | indemnity/ compensation |
| indemnité d'éviction | compensation for eviction |
| indivis | undivided |
| indivision | joint ownership |
| inexécution | breach |
| infiltration | seepage/rising damp |
| ingénieur | engineer |
| inhabité | uninhabited |
| inondation | flood |
| inox | stainless steel |
| inoxydable | rustproof |
| inscription | registration |
| insidieux | creeping |
| insonorisation | sound proofing |
| installation | fittings |
| installation téléphonique | telephone |
| insuffisance | deficiency |
| interdiction | ban/prohibition |

| | |
|---|---|
| inter horaire | time switch |
| intérimaire | interim/temporary |
| intermédiaire | agent/intermediary |
| interphone | entry phone/intercom |
| interrupteur | on/off switch |
| interrupteur va-et-vient | two-way switch |
| interurbain | intercity |
| intimité | privacy |
| intituler | to entitle |
| inventaire | inventory |
| isolant | insulating |
| isolation (phonique/ acoustique/ thermal) | sound/heat insulation |
| isolé | isolated |
| | |
| jalon | landmark/milestone |
| jalousie | slatted blind |
| jardin de rocaille | rock garden |
| jardinière | window box |
| jauge | guage |
| jauge à mazout | fuel guage |
| jeu de clès | set of spanners |
| joint | grouting |
| joint d'étanchéité | draft excluder |
| jointoyer | point brickwork |
| jouissance | enjoyment/ possession |
| jumelée | semi-detached |
| jumelle | semi-detached |
| | |
| lâche | loose |
| laque | lacquer |
| laine d'acier | wire wool |
| laine de verre | fibreglass |
| laiton | brass |
| lambrequin | pelmet |
| lambris | cladding/tongue and groove panelling |
| lampe à souder à gaz | blow lamp |
| lampe de table | table lamp |
| largeur | width |
| latte | batten |
| latté | blockboard |

| | | | |
|---|---|---|---|
| lattis | lathwork | machine à laver | washing machine |
| lavabo | washbasin | maçon | builder/bricklayer |
| lave-mains | hand basin | maçonnerie | masonry |
| laverie | laundry | magnétoscope | video recorder |
| laveur de | window cleaner | maillet | mallet |
| carreaux | | main courante | handrail/bannister |
| lave-vaisselle | dishwasher | mains d'oeuvre | labour/manpower/ |
| lézarde | crack | | workforce |
| libérer | to vacate | maintien | maintenance |
| liège | cork tiling | maire | mayor |
| lien | attachment/link/tie | mairie | town hall |
| limites de terrain | boundary | maison | house |
| lingerie | linen room | maison d'amis | weekend house |
| linteau | lintel | maison de | country house |
| lit | bed | campagne | |
| lit bateau | antique bed | maison de maître | gentleman's house |
| lit de traverse | alcove bed | maison jumelle | semi detached house |
| literie | bedding | maison mère | parent company |
| littoral | coast | maison | farm-house |
| living | living room | paysanne | |
| livrable | available | maisonette | cottage |
| livraison | delivery | majoration | increase/rise/surcharge |
| livrer | to deliver | malfaçon | defect/fault |
| local | community/parish | manchon | sleeve/ |
| locataire | tenant | | straight coupling |
| location | hire/letting | mandat | Power of Attorney/ |
| location meublée | furnished letting | | proxy |
| location | holiday let | mandat de | power given to |
| saisonnière | | recherche | someone to find a |
| locaux vacants | vacant premises | | property |
| logement | accommodation/ | mandataire | authorised agent |
| | dwelling | manoir | manor |
| longueur | length | manteau de | chimney piece |
| loquet | latch | cheminée | |
| loqueteau | door catch/small hinge | marbre | marble |
| lotissement | housing estate | marche | step |
| louer | to hire/let | marquise | porch |
| loué | let | marteau | hammer |
| loyer | rent | marteau à deux | sledge hammer |
| lucarne | dormer window/ | mains | |
| | skylight | marteau de | mechanical hammer |
| lu et approuvé | read and approved | démolition | |
| lumière | light/electric light | marteau | claw hammer |
| lumière de | bedside lamp | d'emballeur | |
| chevet | | mas | farmhouse |
| lumineux | luminous | mastic | putty/filler |
| lustre | gloss | matelas | mattress |

| matelas à ressorts | spring mattress | motopompe | power-driven pump |
| matériaux de construction | building material | moulure | moulding |
| | | mousse | moss |
| mat | matt | multirisque | multi-risk |
| mazout | fuel oil | municipal | borough/civic council |
| mèche à bois/ à beton | wood/concrete drill/bit | mur | wall |
| | | mur de clèture | boundary wall |
| mélangeur | mixer tap | mur mitoyen | party wall |
| mélèze | larch | murs extérieurs | exterior walls |
| mensuel | monthly | muret | low wall |
| menuiserie | joinery | muret en pierre sèche | dry stone wall |
| menuisier | joiner | | |
| menus entretiens | minor repairs | nappe | expanse/layer/sheet |
| menus réparations | minor repairs | nettoyage | cleaning |
| | | nettoyant | cleaning fluid |
| menuiserie | woodwork | neutre | neutral |
| mètre carré | square metre | niveau | level/grade |
| mètre pliant | folding rule | niveau à bulle d'air | spirit level |
| mètre ruban | tape measure | | |
| metreur | quantity surveyor | noix | walnut |
| metreur vérificateur | quantity surveyor | nommer | to appoint |
| | | non-goudronné | unmade (road) |
| mettre à terre | to earth | non-livraison | non-delivery |
| meublé | furnished | non-meublé | unfurnished |
| meuble à demeure | fitment | normes | standards |
| | | note de renseignements d'urbanisime | local authority search |
| meubles | furniture | | |
| meublés classés tourisme | classified tourist accommodation | notaire | notary |
| milieu | environment/middle | notification | notice |
| minuterie | time-switch | | |
| miroir | mirror | occasion | second hand |
| mise en demeure | notice | occultation | overshadowing |
| mitigeurs | mixer tap | occuper | to occupy |
| mitoyen | intermediate | odeur | smell |
| moellons | rubble/quarry stone | oeuvre | work |
| mobilier | furnishings | oléoduc | pipeline |
| mois | month | omettre | to omit |
| moisissure | fungus/mildew | opaque | opaque |
| moquette | fitted carpet | ordinateur | computer |
| morceler | to break up/partition | ordures | rubbish |
| mortier | mortar/grout | oreiller | pillow |
| mortier colle | tile cement | oriel | bow/bay window |
| mortier rapide | quick setting cement | orme | elm |
| mortier réfractaire | heat resistant cement | ortie | nettle |
| mosaïque | mosaic | outil | tool |

| | | | |
|---|---|---|---|
| outillage | equipment/machinery | peinture laquée | enamel |
| outre | in addition to | pelle | shovel |
| ouverture | opening | pelouse | lawn |
| ouvrier | workman | pendule | clock (small) |
| ouvrier maçon | bricklayer | pépinière | garden centre |
| | | perceuse | drill |
| paiement comptant | cash payment | périmé | out of date |
| | | permis de construire | planning permission |
| paillasson | door mat | | |
| paisiblement | peacefully | persienne | blind/slatted shutter |
| pallier | landing | personne physique | individual |
| pâlir | to fade | | |
| palissandre | rosewood | personne morale | company |
| paillasson d'entrée | doormat | perte | loss |
| | | peuplier | poplar |
| panne | breakdown | phase | phase (electrical) |
| papier de verre | sandpaper | pièce | room (kitchen and bathroom not counted) |
| papier peint | wallpaper | | |
| papier préencollé | ready pasted wallpaper | | |
| | | pied-de-biche | claw hammer |
| parcelle | allotment/lot/parcel | pin | pine |
| parking | parking lot | pierre | stone |
| parois | partition walls | pierre concassée | crushed stone |
| paroisse | parish | pignon | gable |
| parpaing | breeze block | pilier | pillar |
| parquet | parquet | pinceau | paintbrush |
| partager | to share/split | pinces | pliers |
| parterre | flower bed | pioche | pickaxe |
| particulier | individual | pipe à sortir | evacuation pipe |
| parties communes | common parts of a building | piquet de terre | earthing pin |
| | | piscine | swimming pool |
| parties privatives | private parts of a building | pistolet | spray gun |
| | | placage | veneer |
| passe-plat | service hatch | placard | built-in cabinet/ cupboard/veneer |
| paumelle | split hinge | | |
| pavage | pavement | place de stationnement | parking space |
| pavé | paving stone | | |
| pavillon | summer house | placoplâtre | plasterboard |
| peindre et tapisser | to decorate | plafond | ceiling/cap |
| | | plain-pied | single storey |
| peine | penalty/sanction/ sentence | plan | chart/plan |
| | | planche | plank/floorboard |
| peintre | painter | planche d'échafaudage | scaffold board |
| peinture | paint/painting | | |
| peinture acrylique | acrylic paint | planchéiage | boarding |
| peinture crépi | masonry paint | plancher | floor boards |
| peinture émulsion | emulsion paint | plan | plan |

| | | | |
|---|---|---|---|
| plaque chauffante | hob/hot plate | poutre | beam |
| plaque d'égout | manhole cover | poutres apparentes | exposed beams |
| platane | plain tree | | |
| plateau | shelf | poutrelle | small beam |
| plate-bande | flower bed | pouvoir | power |
| plâtre | plaster | préavis | notice |
| plâtrier | plasterer | préjudice | damage |
| plâtroir | plastering trowel | prélèvement automatique | standing order |
| plinthe | skirting board | | |
| plomb | lead | premier étage | first floor |
| plomberie | plumbing | preneur | tenant |
| plombier | plumber | prénom | first name |
| plus-value | capital gain | prime | premium |
| poêle | wood-burning stove | prise | electric socket/ power point |
| poignée | handle | | |
| poignée de porte | door handle | prise de terre | earthing point/socket |
| poinçon | awl/bradawl | prix fixé | fixed price |
| police | police/policy | procuration | power of attorney |
| polyvalant | multi-purpose | profondeur | depth |
| pompe | pump | projecteur | floodlight |
| pompe de puisard | sump | projet | draft |
| | | prolongateur | extension lead |
| pompiers | fire brigade | promoteur immobilier | property developer |
| ponceuse | sander | | |
| ponceuse à bande | belt sander | promesse de vente | contract |
| ponceuse vibrante | orbital sander | propre | clean |
| | | propriétaire | owner |
| porche | porch | propriété | property |
| portail | garden gate/gateway | province | country (as opposed to town) |
| porte | door/gate | | |
| porte coulissante | sliding door | provisoire | draft/interim/ provisional/temporary |
| porte va-et-vient | swing door | | |
| porte-fenêtre | French window | proximité | near/proximity |
| porte-blindée | reinforced door | puisard | cesspool/sink/sump |
| porte fusible | fuse box | puissance | capacity/power/ strength/wattage |
| porte vitre | glass door | | |
| portillon | gate | puits | well |
| pose | fix | puits perdu | soakaway |
| pose des vitres | glazing | purger | to clear |
| poste de soudage à l'arc | arc welder | pylône | pylon |
| pot de cheminée | chimney pot | quartier | quarter |
| potager | kitchen garden | queue-d'aronde | dovetail |
| poubelle | dustbin | quincaillerie | hardware/ironmongery |
| poulie | pulley | quinzaine | fortnight |
| pourrissement | rot | quittance | receipt |

| | |
|---|---|
| quitus | discharge |
| quote-part | contribution |
| quotidien | daily |
| | |
| rabot | plane |
| raccord | joint/connection |
| raccord coudé | bend joint |
| raclette | scraper |
| radiateur soufflant | fan heater |
| rainure et longuette | tongue and groove |
| rallonge | extension |
| ramonage | chimney sweeping |
| ramoneur | chimney sweep |
| rampants | roof arches |
| rampe d'escalier | bannister |
| rangements | storage space |
| râpe | rasp |
| rapport d'avant projet | feasibility report |
| rapport d'expertise | loss adjuster's report |
| ravalement | cleaning/restoration |
| rayer | to scratch |
| raz de marée | landslide |
| reboisement | reafforestation |
| rebord de fenêtre | window-sill (inside) |
| réception des travaux | completion of building works |
| réclamation | claim |
| recoin | recess |
| reconduction | renewal |
| rectifier | to amend |
| reçu | receipt |
| rédaction | preparing/drafting |
| redevable | taxpayer |
| redevance | due/fee/tax |
| refait | restored |
| réfectoire | dining room |
| regard de visite | inspection chamber |
| Registre du Commerce et des Sociétés (RCS) | companies registry |

| | |
|---|---|
| réglage de la temperature | temperature control |
| règle | rule/ruler |
| règle niveau | spirit level |
| règlement | payment/settlement |
| règlement de copropriété | lease of the common parts |
| réglet métallique | metal knife |
| remblai | ballast/embankment/hardcore |
| remis à neuf | replacement as new |
| remise | garage/shed/store |
| remise des clefs | handing over of keys |
| renforcer | to reinforce/strengthen |
| renonciation | abandonment/renunciation |
| renouveler | to renew |
| rénové | renovated |
| renseignements | enquiries/information |
| réparation | repair |
| répertoire des métiers | trade register |
| replâtrage | patching up |
| représentant | representative |
| résilier | to cancel/terminate |
| responsabilité civile | civil liability |
| resserrer | to squeeze/lighten |
| restauration | restoration |
| restaurer | to restore |
| restitution des clés | return of the keys |
| rétrécir | to narrow |
| revêtement | new coating or facing surface |
| revêtement de sol | floor covering |
| rez-de-chaussée | ground floor |
| rideau | curtain |
| risque | hazard/risk |
| ristourne | drawback |
| rive de toits | roof edge |
| riverain | riperian/bordering |
| robinet | tap |
| robinet de fermeture | stop cock |
| robinet de purge | air release tap |

| | | | |
|---|---|---|---|
| robinet thermostatique | thermostatic radiator tap | séjour | living room/stay |
| robinetterie | plumbing/taps | semaine | week |
| rondelle | washer | semelle | roofplate |
| rosace | ceiling rose | semestriel | bi-yearly |
| rètissoire | spit | se prendre en glace | freeze up |
| rouille | rust | séquoia | redwood |
| rouleau à peinture | paint roller | serre | conservatory/ glasshouse |
| rubrique | column/heading | serrure | lock |
| ruine | run-down property | serrurier | locksmith |
| ruisseau | stream | service d'eau | water authority |
| rupture | breach | service de ménage | cleaning services |
| SA | corporation | services collectifs | collective services |
| sablager | to sandblast | seuil | sill/threshold |
| sable | sand | siège | seat/registered office |
| sable doux | soft sand | siège pour bébé | baby chair |
| salle à manger | dining room | signal d'incendie | fire alarm |
| salle de bain | bathroom | siphon | water/drain tap |
| salle de séjour | living room | société | company |
| salon | living room/lounge | socle | insulating base |
| sanitaire | sanitary | sol | ground/floor |
| sans cloisons | open plan | solidaire | joint |
| sans effet | void | solidairement | jointly and severally |
| sans littoral | landlocked | solive | joist |
| SARL | limited liability company | sommation | notice |
| | | somme garantie | sum insured |
| sapin | fir | sonnette | door bell |
| saule | willow | sonnerie d'alarme | alarm bell/ burglar alarm |
| sellé | padlock/seal | | |
| SCI | non-trading property holding company | souder | to weld |
| | | soudure | solder |
| scie | saw | soupape | valve |
| scie à chaînette | chainsaw | sous-couche | undercoat |
| scie à métaux | hacksaw | sous-location | sublease |
| scie à chantourner | jig saw | sous-louer | to sublet |
| | | sous seing privé | legal document not registered with a notaire |
| scie à ruban | band saw | | |
| scie à tenon | tenon saw | | |
| scie circulaire | circular saw | sous-sol | basement/underground |
| scie mécanique | circular saw | soussigné | undersigned |
| scie sans fin | band saw | sous-traitance | subcontracting |
| scie sauteuse | jig saw | station d'épuration | purification plant |
| scie vilebrequin | ceramic tile cutting saw | | |
| seau | bucket | statuts | memorandum and articles of association |
| sèche-linge | clothes dryer | | |

| | | | |
|---|---|---|---|
| store | roller blind | toile de jute | hessian |
| store vénitien | venetian blind | toit | roof |
| succession | estate for inheritance purposes | toit en ardoise | slate roof |
| | | toiture | roofing |
| superficie | acreage/area/surface | tôle ondulée | corrugated iron |
| support | prop/bearer | tondeuse | lawn mower |
| surpeuplement | overpopulation | tontine | joint tenancy |
| surplomb | overhang | tournevis | screwdriver |
| syndic | managing agent of a block of flats | tout à l'égout | mains drainage |
| | | travailleur indépendant | self-employed person |
| table à encoller | pasting table | travaux d'amélioration | improvement/ renovation works |
| table de toilette | dressing table | | |
| table de nuit | bedside table | travaux publics | public works |
| tablette | shelf | travaux temporaires | temporary works |
| tablette de cheminée | mantelpiece | | |
| | | treillage | trellis work |
| tabouret | stool | treillis métallique | wire netting |
| tacite reconduction | tacit renewal | treillis soudé | welded steel mesh |
| | | tréteau | trestle |
| taille | size | trimestre | quarter (three months) |
| tapis | rug/carpet | tronçonneuse | chain saw |
| targette | bolt | trop-plein | waste pipe |
| tasseau | bracket | trou | hole/air vent |
| taudis | slum | trou de serrure | keyhole |
| taxe d'habitation | residential tax | trou de sondage | bore hole |
| taxes foncières | land and building taxes | trou de vers | worm hole |
| taxe professionnelle | business tax | trou de visite | manhole |
| | | truelle | trowel |
| taxe de séjour | tax on hotel accommodation | truelle de maçon | masonry trowel |
| | | trumeau | chimney breast |
| teck | teak | tube de cuivre | copper pipe |
| tenon et mortaise | mortise and tenon | tuile | roof tile |
| tension du courant | voltage | tuile de rive | edge tile |
| | | tuyau | tube/pipe |
| terrain | field/ground/land | tuyau d'arrosage | hosepipe |
| terrain à bâtir | building plot | tuyau d'écoulement | drain pipe |
| terre | earth | | |
| terre cuite | unglazed brick/ terracotta | tuyau de descente | down pipe |
| | | | |
| testament | will | tuyau d'égout | soil pipe |
| textile muraux | fabric wall covering | tuyau de vidange | drain pipe |
| tilleul | lime tree | tuyauterie | piping |
| tiroir | drawer | tuyau en PVC | PVC pipe |
| tissu | fabric/cloth | TVA | VAT |
| tissus d'ameublement | furnishing fabrics | | |
| | | urbanisme | town planning |

| | | | |
|---|---|---|---|
| usine | factory | vice de construction | defect in construction |
| ustensiles | utensils | | |
| usufruit | life interest | vidange | draining |
| usufruitier | life tenant | vide-ordures | rubbish bin |
| usure | wear and tear | vilebrequin | bit brace |
| | | villa | detached house |
| vaisselle | crockery/dishes | virement | bank transfer |
| valeur à neuf | value as new | vis | screw |
| valeur de remplacement | replacement value | vis à calotte | mirror screw |
| | | vis à tête fraisée | countersunk screw |
| variateur | dimmer switch | vis à tête ronde | dome headed screw |
| velours | velvet | visite des lieux | site inspection |
| vente | sale | visser | to screw on |
| verger | orchard | vitrage | glazing |
| vermoulu | worm-eaten | vitre | glass/window pane |
| vernis | varnish | vitrier | glazer |
| verre | glass | vitrification | glazing |
| verre à pied | stemmed glass | voie privée | driveway |
| verrou | bolt | voisin | neighbour |
| vers à bois | woodworm | volet | shutter |
| vestibule | entrance hall | volige | thin plank |
| vétusté | wear and tear | voûte | vault |
| vétusté deduite | deduction for wear and tear | voyant | garish/gaudy/loud |
| viabilisé | building site on which the roads have been made | watt | watt |
| | | white-spirit | white spirit |
| vice | defect/flaw | zinc | zinc |
| vices cachés | hidden defects | zone | area/zone |